Smart
Writing

영작문 기초 탄탄하게 잡아주는 Smart Writing 2

지은이 전종삼, 스티브 브라운, 조금배
펴낸이 임상진
펴낸곳 (주)넥서스

출판신고 1992년 4월 3일 제311-2002-2호 ②
10880 경기도 파주시 지목로 5
Tel (02)330-5500 Fax (02)330-5555

ISBN   979-11-5752-556-0   54740
          979-11-5752-554-6 (SET)

가격은 뒤표지에 있습니다.
잘못 만들어진 책은 구입처에서 바꾸어 드립니다.

본 책은 〈Writing Master 2〉의 개정판입니다.

www.nexusEDU.kr
NEXUS Edu는 넥서스의 초·중·고 학습물 전문 브랜드입니다.

영작문 기초 **탄탄하게** 잡아주는

Smart
Writing

전종삼 · 스티브 브라운 · 조금배 지음

2

NEXUS Edu

지은이 소개

전종삼
- 미국 뉴욕 주립대학교 영어교육학 석사
- 한양대학교 TESOL 수료

스티브 브라운
- 영국 증권 투자 위원회 학사
- 미국 앤도버 국제영어학교 TEFL 수료

조금배
- 미국 하와이 퍼시픽 대학교 TESL 석사
- 정이조영어학원 팀장

Introduction

Smart Writing is designed to help you become a better writer. It will teach you about the process of writing. The writing process consists of more than just picking up a pencil and writing a paragraph or an essay from beginning to end. Writing is a process because it goes through many stages. It starts with understanding what is expected of you in a writing assignment. Next, it involves thinking about what you are going to write and planning how you are going to organize it. The final steps involve writing, checking your work, and rewriting. Being a good writer means you continually change, add to, and improve what you have already written.

Sometimes the hardest part of writing is deciding what you are going to say. That is why the models in this book are organized around topics familiar to most people. While you are doing the prewriting activities and reading the models, you should think about the topic and how it relates to you and your life. Then, when it's your time to write, you will have some ideas about what you want to say.

In addition to organization, you will learn other aspects of writing, including punctuation, the use of linking words, and paragraph and essay formats. To become a better writer, you must start with the basics of format and organization.

There are so many people to thank when you write a book like this. Our family members have been very supportive of us. We are also very thankful for all the people giving us precious tips for this book. And, most of all we would like to thank our publisher 'NEXUS.'

We hope that you enjoy using this book and that it helps you improve your English.

Unit structure

Warm-up

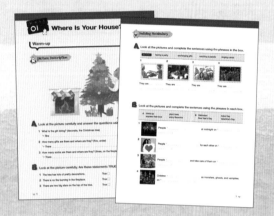

- The "Picture Description" section gets students to look at a picture and answer some simple questions. Students are introduced to words and phrases used in the unit and gain insight into the unit topic.

- The "Building Vocabulary" section provides more words and phrases that are relevant to the unit topic. The words and phrases are used in context to ensure students know how to use them accurately.

Reading and Understanding & Complete the Outline

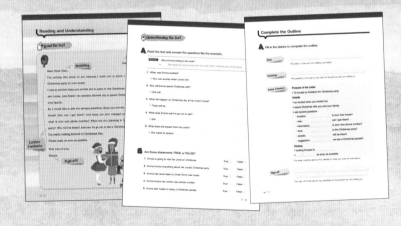

- Students read a passage about the topic in the "Read the Text" section. The passage contains examples of the grammar point that will be studied in the unit, and the passage is structured so that students can use it as a template for their own writing.

- The "Understanding the Text" section makes sure students fully comprehend and understand the passage.

- In "Complete the Outline," the students further reinforce their comprehension of the text and their understanding of the components of different types of writing: essays, letters, presentations, emails etc.

Grammar Point

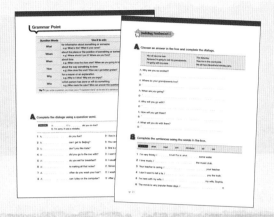

- The "Grammar Point" section explains the grammar topic of the unit. Students reinforce their knowledge of the grammar point via exercises.

- In "Building Sentences," students practice both the sentence structures used in the reading passage and the unit grammar point so that they are ready to write their own text.

Writing

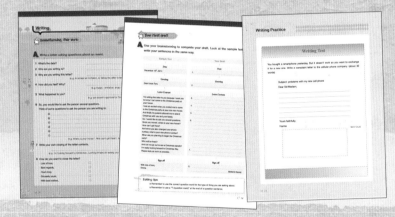

- The "Brainstorming" section guides students to find their own ideas to use in their writing task.

- In "Your First Draft," students use their brainstorming in a guided writing exercise that follows the structure and format of the reading passage.

- In "Writing Practice," students are given the opportunity to practice skills that will be needed in the writing tests.

Workbook

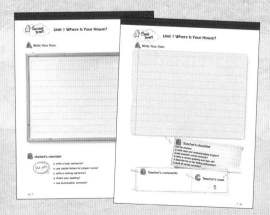

Students revise and edit their first draft, and produce a final draft of their writing task.

Students can write their final draft on their WORKBOOK.

* Answers download at www.nexusEDU.kr

Contents

Plan of the book

unit	Category	Title	Grammar point	Writing task
1	Events	Where Is Your House?	Question Word	Write a Letter
2	Entertainment	Be a Movie Star!	Possessive Case	Write an Advertisement
3	Friends	What My Friends Can Do	Too / Either / Also	Introduce Your Friends
4	Planning	My Busy Schedule	Modal Verbs	Write about Things To Do
5	Nature	Wonderful Spring!	So / Because	Write about Favorite Season
6	Culture	My Home Town	As ~ as Comparative	Write an Essay
7	Politics	A Campaign Speech	First Conditional	Write a Speech
8	Journey	Going Abroad	To Infinitive	Write an Email
9	Science & Technology	My Favorite Website	Gerund	Write an Essay
10	Feelings & Emotions	A Complaint Letter	Many / Much / A lot of	Write a Letter

Unit
01

Where Is Your House?

December 10th , 2014
Dear Uncle Tom,
I'm writing this letter to you because I want you to know I can come to the Christmas party at your house. I was so excited when you invited me to come to the Christmas party at your nice new house. And finally my parents allowed me to spend Christmas with you and your family. So, I would like to ask you several questions. Since you moved, where is your new house? How can I get there? And since you also changed your phone number, what is your new phone number? When are you planning to begin the Christmas party? Who will be there? And can we go out to see a Christmas parade?I'm really looking forward to Christmas Day.Please reply as soon as possible.
With lots of love,
Emma

Where Is Your House?

Warm-up

Picture Description

A Look at the picture carefully and answer the questions using the given words.

1 What is the girl doing? (decorate, the Christmas tree)

↳ She _____ .

2 How many gifts are there and where are they? (five, under)

↳ There _____ .

3 How many socks are there and where are they? (three, on the fireplace)

↳ There _____ .

B Look at the picture carefully. Are these statements TRUE or FALSE?

1 The tree has lots of pretty decorations. True ☐ False ☐

2 There is no fire burning in the fireplace. True ☐ False ☐

3 There are two big stars on the top of the tree. True ☐ False ☐

A Look at the pictures and complete the sentences using the phrases in the box.

| Word Box | having a party | exchanging gifts | watching a parade | singing carols |

1 They are _____ .

2 They are _____ .

3 They are _____ .

4 They are _____ .

B Look at the pictures and complete the sentences using the phrases in each box.

| **A** dress up | plant trees | **B** Halloween | Arbor Day |
| express their love | enjoy fireworks | New Year's Day | Valentine's Day |

1 People ᴬ_____ at midnight on ᴮ_____
_____ .

2 People ᴬ_____ for each other on ᴮ_____
_____ .

3 People ᴬ_____ and take care of them on ᴮ_____
_____ .

4 Children ᴬ_____ as monsters, ghosts, and vampires
on ᴮ_____ .

Reading and Understanding

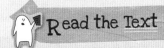

Date

December 10th, 2014

Greeting

Dear Uncle Tom,

I'm writing this letter to you because I want you to know I can come to the Christmas party at your house.

I was so excited when you invited me to come to the Christmas party at your nice new house. And finally my parents allowed me to spend Christmas with you and your family.

So, I would like to ask you several questions. Since you moved, where is your new house? How can I get there? And since you also changed your phone number, what is your new phone number? When are you planning to begin the Christmas party? Who will be there? And can we go out to see a Christmas parade?

I'm really looking forward to Christmas Day.

Please reply as soon as possible.

Letter Contents

With lots of love,

Emma

Sign-off

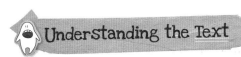

 Read the text and answer the questions like the example.

Example   Why is Emma writing to her uncle?

↘   She wants her uncle to know she can come to the Christmas party at his house.

---

1 When was Emma excited?

↘ She was excited when Uncle Tom _____.

2 Who will Emma spend Christmas with?

↘ She will _____.

3 What will happen on Christmas day at her uncle's house?

↘ There will be _____.

4 What does Emma want to go out to see?

↘ She _____.

5 What does she expect from her uncle?

↘ She wants to receive _____.

Are these statements TRUE or FALSE?

1	Emma is going to visit her uncle on Christmas.	True ☐	False ☐
2	Emma knows everything about her uncle's Christmas party.	True ☐	False ☐
3	Emma has never been to Uncle Tom's new house.	True ☐	False ☐
4	Emma knows her uncle's new phone number.	True ☐	False ☐
5	Emma also hopes to enjoy a Christmas parade.	True ☐	False ☐

Complete the Outline

 Fill in the blanks to complete the outline.

Date ------

_____

: The date is when you are writing your letter.

Greeting ------

_____ ,

: The greeting is the way to say hello to the person you are writing to.

Letter Contents ----

Purpose of the Letter

• To accept an invitation for Christmas party

Details

• so excited when you invited me

• spend Christmas with you and your family

• ask several questions

   - location: _____ is your new house?

   - way: _____ can I get there?

   - information: _____ is your new phone number?

   - time: _____ is the Christmas party?

   - people: _____ will be there?

   - suggestion: _____ we see a Christmas parade?

Closing

• looking forward to _____

• _____ as soon as possible

: The letter contents give us the details of what you want to write about.

Sign-off -----

_____ ,

_____

: The sign-off is the way to say goodbye to the person you are writing to.

Grammar Point

Question Words	Use it to ask:
What	for information about something or someone e.g.) **What** is this? **What** is your name?
Where	about the place or the position of something or someone e.g.) **Where** should I put it? **Where** are you from?
When	about time e.g.) **When** does the class start? **When** are you going to bed?
How	about the way something is done e.g.) **How** does this work? **How** can I get better grades?
Why	for a reason or an explanation e.g.) **Why** is it blue? **Why** are you angry?
Who	which person has done or will do something e.g.) **Who** made the cake? **Who** can answer this question?

Tip ◆ If you write a question, you must use a "? (question mark)" at the end of a sentence.

 Complete the dialogs using a question word.

Example
A: _____Why_____ did you do that?
B: I'm sorry. It was a mistake.

1 A: _____ do you live? 　　　　　B: I live in Los Angeles.

2 A: _____ can I get to Beijing? 　　B: You can take an airplane.

3 A: _____ don't you like Kate? 　　B: She is always rude to me.

4 A: _____ did you go to the zoo with? 　B: I went there with my family.

5 A: _____ do you eat for breakfast? 　B: I usually eat toast and juice.

6 A: _____ is making all that noise? 　B: Simon, he is always so loud.

7 A: _____ often do you wash your hair? 　B: I wash my hair every morning.

8 A: _____ can I play on the computer? 　B: After you finish your homework.

13

Building Sentences 1

A Choose an answer in the box and complete the dialogs.

We will take the train.	This Saturday.
Because I'm going to visit my grandparents.	They live in the countryside.
I'm going with my sister.	We will have Grandma's birthday party.

A: Why are you so excited?

B: ¹ _____

A: Where do your grandparents live?

B: ² _____

A: When are you going?

B: ³ _____

A: Who will you go with?

B: ⁴ _____

A: How will you get there?

B: ⁵ _____

A: What will you do with them?

B: ⁶ _____

B Complete the sentences using the words in the box.

Word Box	~~drink~~	meet	join	introduce	tell	see

1 I'm very thirsty. I ___would like to drink___ some water.

2 I love music. I _____ the music club.

3 Your teacher is caring. I _____ your teacher.

4 I don't want to tell a lie. I _____ you the truth.

5 I'm here with my wife. I _____ my wife, Sophia.

6 The movie is very popular these days. I _____ it.

Building Sentences 2

A Put the words in the correct order to make a sentence.

1 of / the price / the ticket / is / what

↘ _____ ?

2 can't / why / get / a student discount / I

↘ _____ ?

3 is / who / the movie / the main actor / of

↘ _____ ?

4 do / I / to the movie / tickets / buy / how

↘ _____ ?

5 the today's last movie / start / when / does

↘ _____ ?

6 usually go / where / you / to the movies / do

↘ _____ ?

 Complete the letter using the phrases in the box.

Word Box	how can I exchange	reply as soon as	with best wishes
	receiving a new laptop	my laptop has broken	

Dear Mr. Matthew,

I don't feel good because ¹_____. I would like to ask you a

question. ²_____ it for a new one? I'm really looking forward to

³_____ .

Please ⁴_____ possible.

⁵_____ ,

Christine

Writing

Brainstorming ‹Pair Work›

A Write a letter asking questions about an event.

1 What's the date? _____

2 Who are you writing to? _____

3 Why are you writing this letter? _____

          (e.g. to accept an invitation, to refuse the offer, to know about the school trip)

4 How did you feel? Why? _____

          (e.g. happy - invitation, angry - refusal, proud - winning)

5 What happened to you? _____

          (e.g. got parent's approval for Christmas party, won a prize)

6 So, you would like to ask the person several questions.

    Think of some questions to ask the person you are writing to:

    ⓐ _____

    ⓑ _____

    ⓒ _____

    ⓓ _____

    ⓔ _____

    ⓕ _____

       (e.g. Where is your house?, How can I get there?, What is your phone number?)

7 Write your own closing of the letter contents.

    _____

    (e.g. I'm looking forward to Christmas., Looking forward to seeing you., Reply as soon as possible.)

8 How do you want to close the letter?

    - Lots of love, ☐

    - Best regards, ☐

    - Yours truly, ☐

    - Sincerely yours, ☐

    - With best wishes, ☐

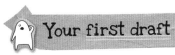

A Use your brainstorming to complete your draft. Look at the sample text and write your sentences in the same way.

Sample Text	Your Draft
Date	**Date**
December 10th, 2014	1. _____
Greeting	**Greeting**
Dear Uncle Tom,	2. _____
Letter Content	**Letter Content**

Sample Text Letter Content:

I'm writing this letter to you because I want you to know I can come to the Christmas party at your house.
I was so excited when you invited me to come to the Christmas party at your nice new house.
And finally my parents allowed me to spend Christmas with you and your family.
So, I would like to ask you several questions. Since you moved, where is your new house?
How can I get there?
And since you also changed your phone number, what is your new phone number?
When are you planning to begin the Christmas party?
Who will be there?
And can we go out to see a Christmas parade?
I'm really looking forward to Christmas Day.
Please reply as soon as possible.

Your Draft Letter Content:
3. _____
4. _____
5. _____
6. _____
7. _____

Sign-off	**Sign-off**
With lots of love, Emma	8. _____
	_____ (Writer's Name)

Editing tips

- Remember to use the correct question word for the type of thing you are asking about.
- Remember to use a "? (question mark)" at the end of a question sentence.

Writing Test

You bought a smartphone yesterday. But it doesn't work so you want to exchange it for a new one. Write a complaint letter to the cellular phone company. (about 30 words)

Subject: problems with my new cell phone

Dear Sir/Madam,

_____

_____

_____

_____

_____

Yours faithfully,

Hanna

Word Count

Be a Movie Star!

Do you want to be a movie star? We are looking for two children for our new movie. We want a girl who is tall and thin, and has long black hair. And the other has to be a boy who is a little chubby and has short blond hair. Both of you must be between 12 and 16. Above all, you must like acting. In the movie, you will play the roles of magic school students. The filming will take place from September through November. So you must be available for three months. Come for an interview at noon on Thursday, the 19th. Please don't be late. To find out more, call us at 3456–7890. This is your chance to be a movie star!

Be a Movie Star!

Warm-up

 Picture Description

The Film of the Year Award Ceremony

A Look at the picture carefully and answer the questions using the given phrases.

1 What are they doing? (come to the Film of the Year Award Ceremony)

↘ They _____ .

2 What is the actress wearing? (a long black dress)

↘ She _____ .

3 What is the man on the right doing? (report about the movie award and movie stars)

↘ He _____ .

B Look at the picture carefully. Are these statements TRUE or FALSE?

1 The actor is wearing a fedora and a bow tie. True ☐ False ☐

2 The child in a tailcoat is waving his hand towards the cameras. True ☐ False ☐

3 Both of the photographers are taking photos. True ☐ False ☐

 Building Vocabulary

A Look at the pictures and complete the signs using the words in the box.

| Word Box | offer | satisfaction | reduced | ~~order~~ | limited |

1 Order Now

2 _____ PRICE

3 _____ GUARANTEE

4 _____ EDITION

5 SPECIAL _____

B Look at the pictures and complete the sentences using the words in each box.

A	**B**	**C**	**D**
short	slender	straight	pale
normal	well-built	curly	lightly tanned
tall	overweight	bald	dark

1

He is a A_____ ,
B_____ man
with a C_____
head. He has D_____
_____ skin.

2

She is A_____
height and has a B_____
_____ figure. She has long
C_____ blond hair.
She has very D_____
_____ skin.

3

He is A_____
and B_____.
He has short, brown C_____
_____ hair. He has D_____
_____ skin.

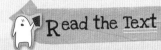

Read the Text

Be a Movie Star!   **Title**

Do you want to be a movie star?   **Topic Sentence**

We are looking for two children for our new movie.

We want a girl who is tall and thin, and has long black hair.

And the other has to be a boy who is a little chubby and has short blond hair.

Both of you must be between 12 and 16. Above all, you must like acting.

In the movie, you will play the roles of magic school students.

The filming will take place from September through November.

So you must be available for three months.

Come for an interview at noon on Thursday, the 19th.

Please don't be late.

To find out more, call us at 3456-7890.

This is your chance to be a movie star!

Advertisement

Closing Sentence   **Contents**

WANTED

Be a Movie Star!

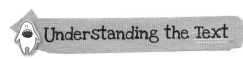

 Read the text and answer the questions like the example.

> **Example**   What is the advertisement about?
>
> ↘ It is _____ a wanted advertisement for child actors _____ .

---

1 Whom are they looking for?

↘ They _____ .

2 What age children can apply for the interview?

↘ The children must be _____ .

3 What role will the children play in the movie?

↘ They _____ .

4 When will the filming take place?

↘ The filming _____ .

5 When is the interview?

↘ At _____ .

Are these statements TRUE or FALSE?

1 They are looking for male actors for their new movie.   True ☐   False ☐

2 They want a girl who has long black hair.   True ☐   False ☐

3 They want a boy who is a little chubby and has short blond hair.   True ☐   False ☐

4 If you want more information, you should email them.   True ☐   False ☐

5 You can be a pop star if you pass the interview.   True ☐   False ☐

Complete the Outline

 Fill in the blanks to complete the outline.

Title ----- Be a _____ !

: The title gives us the topic of the advertisement.

Topic Sentence ----- Do you _____ ?

: The topic sentence in an advertisement should get the readers' attention.

Advertisement Contents -----
Looking for

• two children:

   - a girl: _____, long black hair

                                                  `tall, thin / tall, chubby`

   - a boy: a little _____, short blond hair

                                                  `skinny / chubby`

                                                  `12 and 16 / 13 and 18`

   - age: between _____

   - like _____ `magic / acting`

• the role: _____ students

                                                `art school / magic school`

• when: _____

                    `August through December / September through November`

• Interview day: noon, _____, the 19th

                                                  `Monday / Thursday`

• For more information: _____ us

                                                `call / email`

: The advertisement contents give us the details of the event.

Closing Sentence ----- This is _____ !

: The closing sentence of an advertisement should highlight the benefit of the event.

Grammar Point

> ◉ **We usually use an apostrophe for people and "of" for things and places to make possessive forms.**

	Rules	Examples
people	For singular nouns: -'s	**Sam's** pen is expensive. **Charles's** uncle came to Korea. c.f.) "Charles'" is also possible.
	For plural nouns: i) ending in s: -s' ii) ending in other letters: -'s	The **babies'** beds were all big. The **tigers'** teeth are very strong. **Children's** books have many pictures.
things & places	of+noun	the capital **of Korea** the name **of this building**

 Correct the underlined parts and rewrite the sentences.

1 What are the <u>mens' names</u>?

↳ _____

2 Look at <u>the house's roof</u>.

↳ _____

3 <u>My sister' job</u> is very interesting.

↳ _____

4 Do you know <u>the phone number of Sam</u>?

↳ _____

 Complete the sentences using "-'s" or "of" and the given words.

1 I want to see _____. (Lisa / sister)

2 Do you know _____? (his shoes / the size)

3 _____ was very exciting. (the movie / the end)

4 _____ were hidden in the corner. (the witches / brooms)

5 _____ are Mr. Brown and Ms. Jones. (my teachers / names)

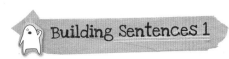

A Look at the pictures and complete the sentences using the given words.

> **Example**
>
> I'm looking for a used car. (a used car)

1 _____ *GAMES*. (a book titled)

2 _____ to my house. (the key)

3 _____ (a parking space)

4 _____ (my pet dog)

B Write sentences like the example.

> **Example** the school festival / on May 20
>
> ⤷ The school festival will take place on May 20.

1 the Academy Awards / on Saturday

⤷ _____

2 the construction / from April through June

⤷ _____

3 the presidential election / on December 19

⤷ _____

4 the next summer Olympic Games / in 2016

⤷ _____

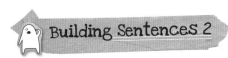

 A Look at the pictures and complete the sentences using the phrases in the box.

Word Box	have a beautiful smile	~~have big eyes~~	are blonde	wear glasses

1
One has brown eyes, and the other has blue eyes.
But _____ both of them have big eyes _____ .

2
One has curly hair, and the other has straight hair.
But _____ .

3
One has an oval face, and the other has a round face.
But _____ .

4
One has fair skin, and the other has dark skin.
But _____ .

 B Complete the advertisement using the phrases in the box.

Word Box	visit our website at	helping the environment	come to the Tong River
	some volunteers to clean	is dying of the waste	help out

Save the Tong River!
The Tong River ¹_____ we throw away.
We are looking for ²_____ the river. You must be fit and like
³_____ . ⁴_____ at 3 p.m. on Saturday.
Food, drinks, trash bags, and gloves are provided. All you have to do is ⁵_____

_____ .
To learn more, ⁶_____ www.tongriver.com.

Writing

Brainstorming ‹Pair Work›

A Create an advertisement.

1 What will you advertise?

_____

(e.g. school play, concert, charity event, job offer)

2 What are you looking for?

_____

(e.g. volunteers, customers, sales staff)

3 What kind of people do you want?

_____

(e.g. fun, active, tall, over 160cm tall, easy-going)

4 What age are you looking for?

_____

(e.g. under 18 years old, over 20 years old, around 30)

5 Above all, what must people do?

_____

(e.g. carry heavy things, sing, smile all day)

6 What will people do at the event?

_____

(e.g. sell things, play games, have fun)

7 When or how long will it take place?

_____

(e.g. September through November, for two months)

8 What must people do to join the event?

_____

(e.g. have an interview, take a test)

9 What else do people have to do?

_____

(e.g. bring a resume, set a date and time for an interview)

10 To find out more, what can people do?

_____

(e.g. call, come to the office, visit the website)

11 Make your own last attractive advertising sentence.

_____

(e.g. This is your chance to be a movie star!, This is your last chance!, Join now!)

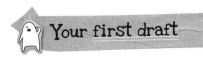
Your first draft

A Use your brainstorming to complete your draft. Look at the sample text and write your sentences in the same way.

Sample Text	Your Draft
Title	**Title**
Be a Movie Star!	
Topic Sentence	**Topic Sentence**
Do you want to be a movie star?	1.
Body	**Body**
We are looking for two children for our new movie. We want a girl who is tall and thin, and has long black hair. And the other has to be a boy who is a little chubby and has short blond hair.	2.
	3.
Both of you must be between 12 and 16. Above all, you must like acting.	4.
In the movie, you will play the roles of magic school students.	5.
	6.
The filming will take place from September through November. So you must be available for three months.	7.
Come for an interview at noon on Thursday, the 19th. Please don't be late.	8.
	9.
To find out more, call us at 3456–7890.	10.
Closing Sentence	**Closing Sentence**
This is your chance to be a movie star!	11.

Editing tips

- Remember to use "?" at the end of a question sentence.
- Remember to use "!" at the end of an exclamation sentence.
- Remember to use a proper punctuation mark at the end of a sentence.

Writing Test

Look at pictures 1 and 2, and describe what you see. Then imagine and write what will happen next. (30~50 words)

①    ②    ③

Word Count

Unit 03

What My Friends Can Do

I would like to introduce some of my talented friends. William is from London. He can play several musical instruments such as the piano, the guitar, and the drums. He has won many musical awards. Kate is also from London. She is a fantastic ice skater, and she is a member of the English national team. Sally is from New York and is good at languages. She can speak three languages fluently. They are English, French, and Spanish. That's why she has many foreign friends. My other talented friend is Peter, from Sydney. He knows lots about electronics, so he sometimes helps people fix their computers. Last time when I was having trouble doing my homework because my computer broke down, he repaired my computer. I couldn't have finished it without his help. I am lucky to have such amazing and skillful friends.

Unit 03 — What My Friends Can Do

Warm-up

Picture Description

William

Rachel

Français

Kate

Peter

Me

 A Look at the pictures carefully and answer the questions.

1 Is William good at playing the piano?

↘ Yes, William has won an award for _____.

2 Is one of the girls practicing ice hockey or ice skating?

↘ She is _____.

3 Has Peter fixed my computer?

↘ Yes, Peter has _____.

B Look at the pictures carefully. Are these statements TRUE or FALSE?

1 One of the girls is reading a Korean book. True ☐ False ☐

2 The boy is playing the piano at the moment. True ☐ False ☐

3 The boy with brown hair is holding a screwdriver. True ☐ False ☐

A Look at the pictures and complete the sentences using the phrases in the box.

Word Box	compose music	design clothes	fix a computer
	solve math problems	make a speech	knit a scarf

1

A boy is pretty good at _____
fixing a computer .

2

A lady is good at _____
_____ .

3

A woman is good at _____
_____ .

4

A man is good at _____
_____ .

5

A girl is good at _____
_____ .

6

A man is good at _____
_____ .

Choose the correct words to complete the sentences.

1 Steve is a (skillful / terrible) barber. He always gives me a nice hair cut.

2 Stephen is a(n) (intelligent / silly) student. He always finishes at the top of the class.

3 Ronaldo is (fantastic / poor) at soccer. He was selected as this season's MVP.

4 Ben is (excellent / no good) at writing. He is a reporter for the school newspaper.

5 Rachel is a (gifted / clumsy) musician. She is a member of the Detroit Philharmonic Orchestra.

6 My aunt is (clever / bad) with a needle and thread. She often makes pretty stuffed animals and gives them to me.

Reading and Understanding

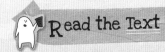
 What My Friends Can Do — Title

Topic Sentence

I would like to introduce some of my talented friends.

William is from London. He can play several musical instruments such as the piano, the guitar, and the drums. He has won many musical awards.

Kate is also from London. She is a fantastic ice skater, and she is a member of the English national team.

Sally is from New York and is good at languages. She can speak three languages fluently. They are English, French, and Spanish. That's why she has many foreign friends.

My other talented friend is Peter, from Sydney. He knows lots about electronics, so he sometimes helps people fix their computers. Last time when I was having trouble doing my homework because my computer broke down, he repaired my computer. I couldn't have finished it without his help.

I am lucky to have such amazing and skillful friends.

Body

Closing Sentence

A Read the text and answer the questions like the example.

Example	Who would you like to introduce?

↘ I _____ would like to introduce some of my talented friends .

1 What can William do?

↘ He _____ .

2 Where do William and Kate come from?

↘ They both _____ .

3 How many languages can Sally speak?

↘ She _____ .

4 What did Peter do for you?

↘ He _____ .

5 Why are you lucky?

↘ I am lucky _____ .

B Are these statements TRUE or FALSE?

1 William knows how to play musical instruments.   True ☐   False ☐

2 Kate is part of the English national dancing team.   True ☐   False ☐

3 Sally is not able to speak Spanish.   True ☐   False ☐

4 Sally has many friends from other countries.   True ☐   False ☐

5 William knows a lot about electronics.   True ☐   False ☐

Complete the Outline

 Fill in the blanks to complete the outline.

Title ---- What My Friends Can Do

: The title gives us the topic of the essay.

Topic Sentence ---- I would like to _____ .

: The topic sentence gives us the main idea of the essay.

Body ----

William
- from London
- plays several _____
- won _____

Kate
- from London
- a fantastic _____
- a member of _____

Sally
- from New York
- speaks _____ fluently
- has _____

Peter
- from Sydney
- knows _____
- helps _____

: The body of the essay gives us the details about the topic.

Closing Sentence ---- I am lucky to _____ .

: The closing sentence finishes the essay. It can be a statement or an opinion.

Grammar Point

too	• Use "too" to add agreement in a positive sentence, and "too" usually comes at the end of a sentence. e.g.) A: I'm happy. B: I am happy, **too**.
either	• Use "either" to add agreement in a negative sentence, and "either" usually comes at the end of a sentence. e.g.) A: I'm not happy. B: I'm not (happy), **either**.
also	• Use "also" to add agreement in a positive sentence, and "also" usually comes after a be verb and a modal verb, and before the other verbs. e.g.) A: I'm from Atlanta. A: Jacob comes from Paris. B: Really? I am **also** from Atlanta. B: Janet **also** comes from Paris.

 Correct the errors in the underlined sentences and rewrite the sentences.

1 I can't play golf. <u>He can't play golf, too.</u>

↳ _____

2 Bill is late for work. <u>John also is late for work.</u>

↳ _____

3 Jim doesn't listen to music. <u>He doesn't watch TV, too.</u>

↳ _____

4 Mr. Jackson is a police officer. <u>His brother is a police officer, either.</u>

↳ _____

5 Jane usually eats lunch at a cafeteria. <u>I eat also lunch at a cafeteria.</u>

↳ _____

6 This dish has a good taste. <u>It is very good for our health, either.</u>

↳ _____

Building Sentences 1

 A Complete the sentences using the phrases in the box.

Word Box	play several musical instruments	repair some electronic equipment
	~~make some food~~	speak several languages fluently
	play several sports	

1 She ___can make some food such as___ spaghetti, pizza, and sandwiches.

2 He _____ the cello, the piano, and the flute.

3 He _____ soccer, baseball, golf, and tennis.

4 He _____ televisions, radios, and computers.

5 She _____ Korean, Japanese, Chinese, and English.

B Look at the pictures and complete the sentences like the example.

Example

I ___help Mom clean the room___ .
(clean the room, Mom)

1 John _____ .
(wash the dishes, her)

2 Claire _____ .
(do his homework, him)

3 Steve _____ .
(fix the computer, her)

4 My grandma _____ .
(knit a scarf, me)

Building Sentences 2

A Look at the pictures and complete the sentences like the example.

Example

I _____ have trouble getting up early in the morning _____ .
(get up early in the morning)

1

I _____ .
(sleep at night)

2

I _____ .
(remember names)

3

×n = 24

I _____ .
(solve this math question)

4

I _____ .
(concentrate on my studies)

B Complete the essay using the phrases in the box.

Word Box	is good at several sports	a member of	I am lucky to have
	my other talented friend is	would like to tell you	won a lot of awards

I ¹_____ about some of my talented friends.
Edward is from Chicago. He ²_____ such as soccer, golf, and
basketball. He has ³_____ .
Sue is also from Chicago. She is a wonderful dancer, and she is ⁴_____
the Chicago Dance Club.
⁵_____ Tony, from New York. He knows lots about history, so he
sometimes helps me with my history homework.
⁶_____ such amazing friends.

Writing

Brainstorming ‹Pair Work›

A Write about what your friends can do.

1 Whom would you like to introduce? _____

(e.g. some of my nice friends, some of my best friends)

What is your friend's name?	Where is he/she from? (e.g. Busan, Seoul, New York, Tokyo)	What can he/she do? (e.g. swim very well, write songs)	What is the result of his/her talent? (e.g. won many awards, is a member of the national team)
2 _____	_____	_____ _____ _____	_____ _____ _____
3 _____	_____	_____ _____ _____	_____ _____ _____
4 _____	_____	_____ _____ _____	_____ _____ _____
5 _____	_____	_____ _____ _____	_____ _____ _____

6 How do you feel to have such amazing and skillful friends?

_____

(e.g. lucky, happy, proud)

A Use your brainstorming to complete your draft. Look at the sample text and write your sentences in the same way.

Sample Text	Your Draft
Title	**Title**
What My Friends Can Do	What My Friends Can Do
Topic Sentence	**Topic Sentence**
I would like to introduce some of my talented friends.	1. _____
Body	**Body**
William is from London. He can play several musical instruments such as the piano, the guitar, and the drums. He has won many musical awards.	2. _____
Kate is also from London. She is a fantastic ice skater, and she is a member of the English national team.	3. _____
Sally is from New York and is good at languages. She can speak three languages fluently. They are English, French, and Spanish. That's why she has many foreign friends.	4. _____
My other talented friend is Peter, from Sydney. He knows lots about electronics, so he sometimes helps people fix their computers. Last time when I was having trouble doing my homework because my computer broke down, he repaired my computer. I couldn't have finished it without his help.	5. _____
Closing Sentence	**Closing Sentence**
I am lucky to have such amazing and skillful friends.	6. _____

Editing tips

* Make sure you use good adjectives to describe what your friends can do.
* Make sure you include something that happened because of your friend's talent. (e.g. He is good at swimming, so he won the gold medal.)
* Make sure you write strong topic and closing sentences.

Writing Practice

Writing Test

Look at the picture carefully and describe what the people are doing.

There are some people at a swimming pool.

A man in a red swimming cap _____(1)_____.

A man in a blue swimming suit _____(2)_____.

A woman in a black swimming cap _____(3)_____.

A woman with sunglasses _____(4)_____.

Word Count

(1)

(2)

(3)

(4)

Unit 04

My Busy Schedule

I have a lot of things to do today. First, I must help Mom throw away the trash. Second, I have to do my English homework. Third, I should clean my room because it is very dirty now. In addition, I need to sort out my clothes because we will have a garage sale this weekend. And I ought to practice the violin for the school contest. Above all, I must do an important thing today before I go to bed. I have a final exam tomorrow, so I must study math. I had better start studying straight away. I have so many things to do today that I don't have time to hang out with my friends.

Unit 04 My Busy Schedule

Warm-up

picture Description

A Look at the picture carefully and answer the questions using the given words.

1 What is the boy doing in the room? (make a list of things to do)

↳ He _____ .

2 What does the boy seem to do for his father? (mow the lawn)

↳ He _____ for his father.

3 What subject does the boy have to study? (English)

↳ He _____ .

B Look at the picture carefully. Are these statements TRUE or FALSE?

1 The boy is thinking about things that he needs to do. True ☐ False ☐

2 The boy has to practice the cello after school. True ☐ False ☐

3 The boy will help Mom wash the dishes. True ☐ False ☐

A Fill in the blanks using the words in the box.

Word Box	midday	midnight	dusk	dawn

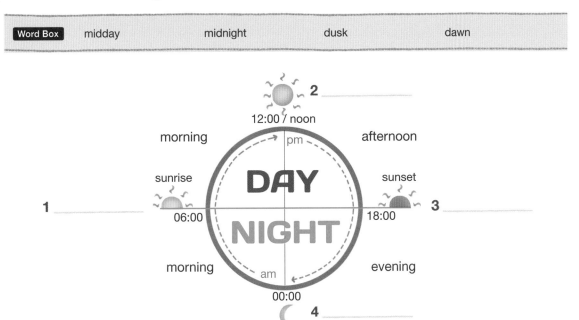

B Look at the pictures and write sentences using the phrases in the box.

Word Box	check out some books	do my assignment	~~go to a ballet lesson~~
	pick up dry cleaning	get a haircut	go to the dentist

1   I have to go to a ballet lesson.

2

3

4

5

6

Reading and Understanding

 Read the **T**ext

My Busy Schedule   Title

I have a lot of things to do today.   Topic Sentence

First, I must help Mom throw away the trash. Second, I have to do my English homework. Third, I should clean my room because it is very dirty now. In addition, I need to sort out my clothes because we will have a garage sale this weekend. And I ought to practice the violin for the school contest.

Above all, I must do an important thing today before I go to bed. I have a final exam tomorrow, so I must study math. I had better start studying straight away.

I have so many things to do today that I don't have time to hang out with my friends.

Closing Sentence

Body

Final Exam

Do to list
☐ help throw trash
☐ do English homework
☐ clean my room
☐ sort out my clothes
☐ practice the violin
☑ study math

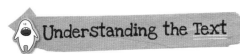

A Read the text and answer the questions like the example.

Example   Why are you so busy today? (today, things, a lot of, to do, have)

↘ Because I _____ have a lot of things to do today _____ .

---

1 What do you have to do? (homework, do, my, have to, English)

↘ I _____ .

2 Why should you clean your room? (very, it, dirty, is)

↘ Because _____ now.

3 What do you need to do with your clothes? (sort out, to, need, my clothes)

↘ I _____ .

4 What musical instrument should you practice for the school contest?
(the contest, should, the violin, practice, for)

↘ I _____ .

5 What must you do before you go to bed and why?
(tomorrow, have, study, a final exam, math, must)

↘ I _____ because I _____ .

B Are these statements TRUE or FALSE?

1 My dad tells me to throw away the trash.   True ☐   False ☐

2 I'm going to sell my used clothes in a garage sale.   True ☐   False ☐

3 I will participate in the violin contest.   True ☐   False ☐

4 I will start studying math as soon as I finish writing my to do list.   True ☐   False ☐

5 After I finish all of the things to do, I will meet and play with my   True ☐   False ☐
friends today.

Complete the Outline

 Fill in the blanks to complete the outline.

Title ----- My Busy Schedule

: The title gives us the topic of the essay.

Topic Sentence ----- I have _____ .

: The topic sentence gives us the main idea of the essay.

Body ----- What to do:

• to _____

help Mom throw away the trash / help Dad clean the house

• to _____

do my science homework / do my English homework

• to _____   clean my room / do the laundry
  - reason: dirty

• to _____   sort out my clothes / do the dishes
  - reason: a garage sale

• to _____   practice the piano / practice the violin
  - reason: the contest

• to _____   study English / study math
  - reason: a final exam

: The body of the essay gives us the details about the topic.

Closing Sentence ----- I have so many things to do today that _____

_____ .

: The closing sentence finishes the essay. It can be a statement or an opinion.

Grammar Point

We use "must," "have to," "had better," "ought to," and "should" to say that an action is necessary.

The degree of necessity: must (have to) > had better > ought to > should

Types	Rules	Examples
Affirmative	modals + base verb	He **should be** quiet in the library.

Negatives	i) must not [=mustn't] + base verb
	  had better not + base verb
	  should not [=shouldn't] + base verb
	  ought not [=oughtn't] to + base verb
	 ⇨ An action is not allowed.
	
	ii) don't [doesn't] have to + base verb
	 ⇨ An action is not necessary.
		You **must not eat** many candies.
		You **had better not go** to bed late.
		He **should not cut** in line.
		They **ought not to miss** the first train.
		
		You **don't have to** take the bus.

Questions	Must/Should + subject + base verb Ought + subject + to + base verb Do/Does + subject + have to + base verb	**Must** we **get** up early? **Ought** I **to tell** Mom? **Do** I **have to write** it down?

 Put the words in the correct order to complete the sentences like the example.

Example	have to / in order to / wake up early / go to school
	↘ I _____ have to wake up early in order to go to school _____ .

1 should / don't know / make a list / what to do next

↘ I _____ , so I _____ .

2 my room / on the computer / should / to play / clean

↘ I want _____ , but I _____ .

3 scared / the dentist / ought to / a bit / visit

↘ I _____ , but I'm _____ .

4 play / be able to / finish / tennis / everything

↘ After I _____ , then I may _____ .

Building Sentences 1

 A Look at the pictures and complete the sentences using the phrases in the box.

| Word Box | make her bed | vacuum the floor | set the table |
| | do the laundry | take out the trash | water the plants |

1

A girl _is making her bed_

_____ .

2

A woman _____

_____ .

3

A man _____

_____ .

4

A woman _____

_____ .

5

A lady _____

_____ .

6

A man _____

_____ .

B Complete the sentences using the phrases in the box.

| Word Box | take a day off | go to bed early | leave now | write them down | stop eating |

1 You have no time. You ____ had better leave now ____ , or you'll be late.

2 I stayed up late yesterday. I _____ tonight.

3 I always forget what things I need to buy. I _____ .

4 I have gained so much weight. I _____ greasy food.

5 You have worked so hard lately. You _____ and rest.

Building Sentences 2

A
Complete the dialogs using the given modals and the words or phrases in the box.

| Word Box | go and see | take an umbrella | buy | park | be careful |

1 A: I have a terrible headache again today.

B: Again? I think you _____ a doctor. (ought to)

2 A: Look at the floor. It's all wet.

B: Yeah, I can see the warning. We _____. (should)

3 A: Look, Sally! There's a parking spot.

B: Don't you see the sign? We _____ our car there. (must, not)

4 A: Do we need to buy some bread?

B: No. We _____ it. We have some at home. (have to, not)

5 A: Mom, I'm going out now!

B: David, it seems like it's going to rain soon. You _____. (had better)

B
Complete the essay using the phrases in the box.

| Word Box | enjoy myself | ought to pack my suitcase | must confirm my flight |
| | had better complete | should exchange some money | have to request |

I have a lot of things to do before going on a vacation.

First, I ¹ _____ and hotel reservation.

Second, I ² _____ to euros. Third, I have to check the weather of my destination.

In addition, I ³ _____ according to the weather.

But above all, I ⁴ _____ a vacation leave. I ⁵ _____ a vacation request form and submit it to the manager right away.

After finishing these things, all I have to do is ⁶ _____ on my vacation.

Writing

 Brainstorming ‹Pair Work›

A Write your list to-do.

1 Why are you so busy today?

_____

(e.g. a lot of things to do, tight schedule, the school project)

2 Make a list of things to do today.

- First, _____

(e.g. to study English, to clean my room, to do the laundry, to write a report)

- Second, _____

(e.g. to study English, to clean my room, to do the laundry, to write a report)

- Third, _____

(e.g. to study English, to clean my room, to do the laundry, to write a report)

- In addition, _____

(e.g. to study English, to clean my room, to do the laundry, to write a report)

- And _____

(e.g. to study English, to clean my room, to do the laundry, to write a report)

3 Above all, what is the most important thing to do? Why?

Above all, _____

(e.g. to write a report - to have to submit, to study hard - to take a test tomorrow,
to practice the piano - to participate in the contest)

4 Talk about what you cannot do because of your busy schedule.

_____

(e.g. cannot go to see a movie, cannot hang out with my friends, cannot go to an amusement park)

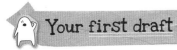**Your first draft**

A Use your brainstorming to complete your draft. Look at the sample text and write your sentences in the same way.

Sample Text	Your Draft
Title	**Title**
My Busy Schedule	My Busy Schedule
Topic Sentence	**Topic Sentence**
I have a lot of things to do today.	1.
Body	**Body**
First, I must help Mom throw away the trash. Second, I have to do my English homework. Third, I should clean my room because it is very dirty now. In addition, I need to sort out my clothes because we will have a garage sale this weekend. And I ought to practice the violin for the school contest. Above all, I must do an important thing today before I go to bed. I have a final exam tomorrow, so I must study math. I had better start studying straight away.	2. 3.
Closing Sentence	**Closing Sentence**
I have so many things to do today that I don't have time to hang out with my friends.	4.

Editing tips
- Remember that "must" and "should" are not followed by "to."
- Make sure your list is in a logical order. (e.g. You cannot go outside until you are dressed!)

Writing Practice

Writing Test

One of your friends broke his leg while skiing and had an operation. He is in the hospital now. Write a get-well-soon letter to him. (about 30 words)

Subject: Hope you feel better soon!

Hi, Jacob!

_____

_____

_____

_____

_____

_____

Sammy

Word Count

Unit 05

Wonderful Spring!

Q: What is your favorite season?
A: My favorite season is definitely spring.
Spring is a wonderful season because nature starts to bloom. The trees and plants get their leaves, so everything becomes green. However, sometimes there is a lot of light rain in spring, and because of this, people need to carry an umbrella. The air in spring feels clean and fresh because spring follows winter. In spring, the weather is not cold, and the sky is often clear. So it is a good time for people to enjoy going on a picnic and hiking. People can also see beautiful flowers everywhere. Spring is a happy and cheerful season because nature is alive, so people should be active and full of life.

Unit 05 · Wonderful Spring!

Warm-up

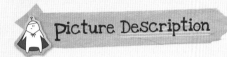
picture Description

 A Look at the pictures carefully and fill in the blanks using the phrases in the box.

Word Box	make a sandcastle	play ice hockey	fly a kite	go on a picnic

1 What are the girls doing in picture A?

↳ They are _____.

2 What are the boys doing in picture B?

↳ They are _____ on the beach.

3 What is the boy in blue overalls doing in picture C?

↳ He is _____ in the field.

4 What are the boys doing in picture D?

↳ They are _____ on the frozen pond.

A Look at the pictures and fill in the blanks using the words in the box.

Word Box	snowstorm	frost	breeze	mist
	dew	shower	tornado	hailstones

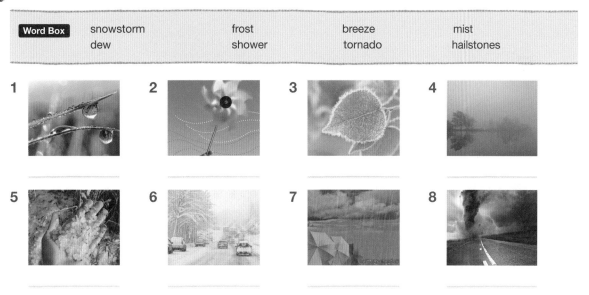

1 _____

2 _____

3 _____

4 _____

5 _____

6 _____

7 _____

8 _____

B Look at the pictures and complete the sentences using the phrases in the box.

Word Box	grow thick	fall down	sprout into buds
	~~plant seeds~~	bear fruit	produce flowers

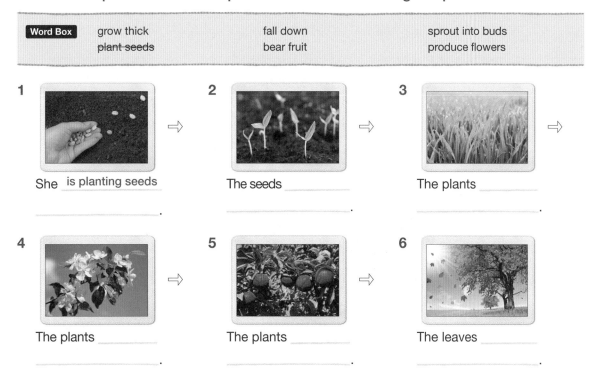

1 She _is planting seeds_ .

2 The seeds _____ .

3 The plants _____ .

4 The plants _____ .

5 The plants _____ .

6 The leaves _____ .

Reading and Understanding

Read the **T**ext

Q: What is your favorite season?

Question

A: My favorite season is definitely spring.

Topic Sentence

Spring is a wonderful season because nature starts to bloom. The trees and plants get their leaves, so everything becomes green. However, sometimes there is a lot of light rain in spring, and because of this, people need to carry an umbrella. The air in spring feels clean and fresh because spring follows winter. In spring, the weather is not cold, and the sky is often clear. So it is a good time for people to enjoy going on a picnic and hiking. People can also see beautiful flowers everywhere.

Spring is a happy and cheerful season because nature is alive, so people should be active and full of life.

Closing Sentence

Body

A Read the text and answer the questions like the example.

Example What is your favorite season?

↘ _My favorite season is definitely spring._

1 Why is spring a wonderful season?

↘ It is wonderful because _____ .

2 Why does everything become green?

↘ Because the trees and plants _____ .

3 Why do people need to carry an umbrella in spring?

↘ Sometimes there is _____ .

4 Why does the air feel clean and fresh?

↘ Because _____ .

5 Why is spring a good time for people to enjoy going on a picnic?

↘ In spring, the weather is _____ .

B Are these statements TRUE or FALSE?

1 In spring, it hardly rains, so it is very dry.　　True ☐　　False ☐

2 People need an umbrella in case of sudden rain.　　True ☐　　False ☐

3 The air in spring often feels heavy and humid.　　True ☐　　False ☐

4 Spring is a good season for going on a picnic.　　True ☐　　False ☐

5 Flowers bloom, and people can enjoy them in spring.　　True ☐　　False ☐

Complete the Outline

 Fill in the blanks to complete the outline.

Question ------ What is your favorite season?

: The question is used to ask for someone's opinion or information.

Answer

Topic Sentence ------ My favorite season is _____.

: The topic sentence gives us the main idea of the essay.

Body ------ Spring

- nature: _____

    starts to bloom / starts to wither

- trees and plants: _____

    become red / become green

- a lot of light rain: _____

    carry an umbrella / carry a jacket

- the air: _____   hot and humid / clean and fresh

- the weather: _____   not cold / not warm

- the sky: _____   often dark / often clear

- people: _____   staying at home / going on a picnic

: The body of the essay gives us the details about the topic.

Closing Sentence ------ _____

_____

: The closing sentence finishes the essay. It can be a statement or an opinion.

Grammar Point

So: used with results/consequences	Because (of): used with cause/reason
so + clause	because + clause because of + noun phrase
- I was sick, **so** <u>I couldn't do my homework</u>. - Kyle didn't have enough sleep, **so** <u>he is sleepy</u>.	- **Because** <u>he was tired</u>, he went to bed early. - He went to bed early **because** <u>he was tired</u>. - **Because of** <u>heavy rain</u>, the game was canceled.

 Combine the sentences using "so" or "because."

Example   We canceled the hike. + It rained.

↳ _____We canceled the hike because it rained._____

---

1   I was tired. + I worked all day.

↳ _____

2   I woke up late. + I need to hurry up.

↳ _____

3   It was very cold. + I closed the window.

↳ _____

4   He works very hard. + He wants to make money.

↳ _____

5   The elevator was out of order. + I took the stairs.

↳ _____

6   He couldn't ride the roller coaster. + He was not tall enough.

↳ _____

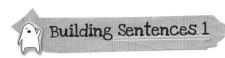
A Look at the pictures and complete the sentences using the given words.

1. Because of heavy rain, _we need to wear rain boots_ .
   (rain boots)

2. Because of yellow dust, _____ .
   (a mask)

3. Because of hot weather, _____ .
   (shorts, a T-shirt)

4. Because of cold weather, _____ .
   (a scarf, gloves, a cap)

5. Because of strong sunlight, _____ .
   (a hat, sunglasses)

 B Complete the essay using the phrases in the box.

Word Box	becomes hotter	goes down below freezing	begins to melt
	become warmer	the first frost appears	see snow everywhere
	feel cooler at night	experience thunderstorms	

In spring, winter snow ¹_____ . The days ²_____
and longer, and the nights remain cool.

In summer, the weather ³_____ . The air is humid, and we often ⁴_____

_____ .

In fall, ⁵_____ . The days become shorter, and we can ⁶_____

_____ .

In winter, the temperature often ⁷_____ . We can also ⁸_____

_____ .

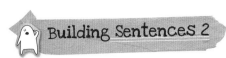

A Look at the pictures and complete the sentences like the example.

Example

Spring is ___a good time for people to go on a picnic___ .
(go on a picnic)

1 Spring is _____ .
(plant trees)

2 Summer is _____ .
(enjoy sunbathing on the beach)

3 Fall is _____ .
(harvest fruit and grain)

4 Winter is _____ .
(go skiing and skating)

B Complete the essay using the phrases in the box

Word Box	enjoy colorful scenery	the best of the year	turn into golden brown
	too hot nor too cold	are amazing	lose all their leaves

My favorite season is fall.

The weather in fall is [1] _____ because it is neither [2] _____

_____ . At the beginning of fall, the colors on the trees [3] _____ .

The leaves [4] _____ and deep red colors, so it looks really beautiful.

But fall is also a little bit sad. Eventually the trees [5] _____ , and we

know winter is coming.

Fall is a great season because the weather is nice, so people can [6] _____ .

 Brainstorming ‹Pair Work›

A Write about your favorite season.

1 What is your favorite season? _____

2 Why do you like this season? _____

(e.g. nature starts to bloom, sunbathing, beautiful scenery, winter sports)

3 What do the trees and plants look like? _____

(e.g. become green, grow thick, turn yellow and red, covered in snow, look white)

4 However, what is a bad thing about this season? _____

(e.g. too much snow, a lot of rain, unpredictable weather, too hot and humid)

5 What do people need to do because of this bad thing?

_____

(e.g. carry an umbrella, wear a hat, carry a warm jacket, be careful when walking or driving)

6 What is the air like in this season? Why? _____

(e.g. clean and fresh - spring follows winter, hot and humid - it rains a lot)

7 What is the weather and the sky like in this season?

_____

(e.g. not cold - sometimes cloudy, freezing - always dark)

8 So, what do people enjoy in this season? _____

(e.g. going on a picnic, going to the beach, going mountain climbing, staying indoors, skiing, skating)

9 What else can they do? _____

(e.g. see beautiful flowers, swim, relax, watch TV, play games, see beautiful scenery)

10 What is your overall opinion about this season? Why?

_____

(e.g. a happy and cheerful season - nature is alive, an active and exciting season - the flowers are everywhere)

11 So, what should people do? _____

(e.g. be active and full of life, stay at home, wear warm clothes)

Your first draft

A Use your brainstorming to complete your draft. Look at the sample text and write your sentences in the same way.

Sample Text	Your Draft
Question	**Question**
What is your favorite season?	What is your favorite season?
Topic Sentence	**Topic Sentence**
My favorite season is definitely spring.	1.
Body	**Body**
Spring is a wonderful season because nature starts to bloom.	2.
The trees and plants get their leaves, so everything becomes green.	3.
However, sometimes there is a lot of light rain in spring, and because of this, people need to carry an umbrella.	4, 5.
The air in spring feels clean and fresh because spring follows winter.	6.
In spring, the weather is not cold, and the sky is often clear.	7. 8.
So it is a good time for people to enjoy going on a picnic and hiking.	9.
People can also see beautiful flowers everywhere.	
Closing Sentence	**Closing Sentence**
Spring is a happy and cheerful season because nature is alive, so people should be active and full of life.	10, 11.

Editing tips

- Make sure you know the difference between "so," "because," and "because of."
- Try to use good adjectives to describe your favorite season.
- Make sure you include descriptions of the weather, temperature, and sky in your draft.

Writing Practice

Writing Test

Look at pictures 1 and 2, and describe what you see. Then imagine and write what will happen next. (30~50 words)

Word Count

Unit 06

My Hometown

I live in a city called Auckland, the biggest city in New Zealand. Auckland is a great place to live in. In Auckland, there are three main attractions: a small but fantastic zoo, the tallest structure called Sky Tower, and a huge park called Auckland Domain. However, my favorite part is Westhaven Marina because its landscape is beautiful. It is also known as the "City of Sails" because there are a lot of boats. Even though there is so much to do, it is also a quiet place to live in. At night, Auckland becomes as quiet as a mouse, so it is easy to rest and relax in. I would recommend that you visit Auckland as soon as possible because it is a clean, exciting, and friendly city.

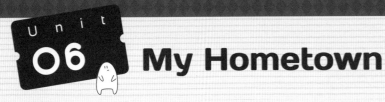
Warm-up

 Picture Description

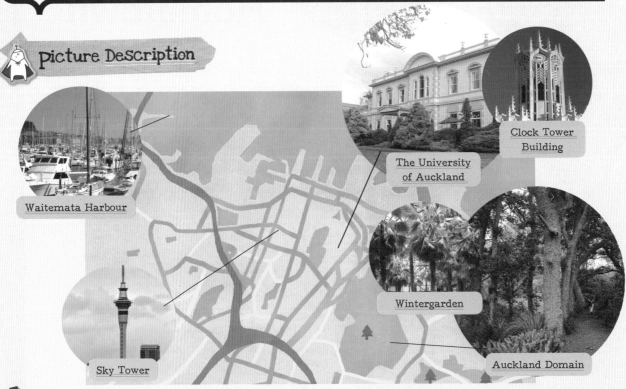

Clock Tower Building

The University of Auckland

Waitemata Harbour

Wintergarden

Sky Tower

Auckland Domain

A Look at the picture carefully and answer the questions like the example.

Example	What is the tallest thing in Auckland? (Sky Tower)
	Sky Tower is the tallest thing in Auckland.

1 What is one of the most famous buildings at the University of Auckland? (the clock tower building)

> _____

2 Are there many boats in Waitemata Harbour?

> Yes. _____

3 Is there a beautiful garden in Auckland Domain?

> Yes. _____

4 What is near Auckland Domain? (the University of Auckland)

> _____

A Look at the pictures and complete the sentences using the words in the box.

Word Box   sidewalk   crosswalk   speed bump   highway   signpost   traffic jam

1

The _____ tells the way to the zoo.

2

I'm stuck in a _____.

3

They are crossing at the _____.

4

A man is driving on the _____.

5

You should slow down at the _____.

6

A man is walking down the _____.

B Look at the pictures and complete the sentences using the phrases in the box.

Word Box   get some rest   buy groceries   spend holidays   eat out

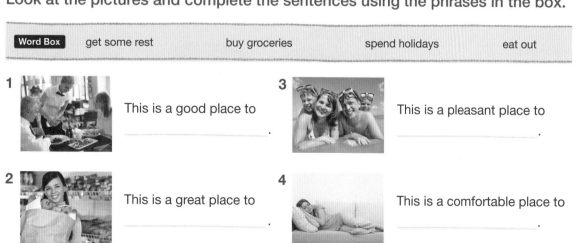

1

This is a good place to _____.

3

This is a pleasant place to _____.

2

This is a great place to _____.

4

This is a comfortable place to _____.

Read the Text

 My Hometown · Title

Topic Sentence

I live in a city called Auckland, the biggest city in New Zealand.

Auckland is a great place to live in.

In Auckland, there are three main attractions: a small but fantastic zoo, the tallest structure called Sky Tower, and a huge park called Auckland Domain.

However, my favorite part is Westhaven Marina because its landscape is beautiful. It is also known as the "City of Sails" because there are a lot of boats.

Even though there is so much to do, it is also a quiet place to live in. At night, Auckland becomes as quiet as a mouse, so it is easy to rest and relax in.

I would recommend that you visit Auckland as soon as possible because it is a clean, exciting, and friendly city.

Closing Sentence

Body

 I ♥ AUCKLAND

A Read the text and answer the questions like the example.

> **Example**   Where is Auckland?
>
> ↘ It _____ is in New Zealand _____.

1 What city do you live in?

↘ I _____.

2 How many main attractions are there in Auckland?

↘ There _____.

3 What is Auckland Domain?

↘ It _____.

4 What is your favorite part of Auckland?

↘ My favorite part of Auckland _____.

5 Why is Westhaven Marina known as the "City of Sails"?

↘ Because _____.

B Are these statements TRUE or FALSE?

1 Auckland is a good place to enjoy a quiet life at night.　　True ☐　　False ☐

2 Auckland is bigger than any other city in New Zealand.　　True ☐　　False ☐

3 There are not many things to do in Auckland.　　True ☐　　False ☐

4 There is a huge and fantastic zoo in Auckland.　　True ☐　　False ☐

5 No structure in Auckland is taller than Sky Tower.　　True ☐　　False ☐

Complete the Outline

 Fill in the blanks to complete the outline.

Title ------- My Hometown

: The title gives us the topic of the essay.

Topic Sentence ------- I live in _____.

: The topic sentence gives us the main idea of the essay.

Body -------
- a great place to live in
  - three main attractions:
    » a _____ zoo 　large / small but fantastic
    » the _____ structure, Sky Tower 　tallest / shortest
    » a _____ park, Auckland Domain 　huge / small
- my favorite place
  - Westhaven Marina, the " _____ "
    City of Snow / City of Sails
  - because of _____
    beautiful landscape / fun activities
- a quiet place to live in
  - _____
    as quiet as a mouse / as busy as a bee
  - _____
    good to sightsee in / easy to rest and relax in

: The body of the essay gives us the details about the topic.

Closing Sentence ------- I would recommend that _____
_____.

: The closing sentence finishes the essay. It can be a statement or an opinion.

Grammar Point

We use "as + adjective/adverb + as" to say that two things or people are the same in some ways.

Rules	Examples
as + adjective + as as + adverb + as	Seoul is **as large as** London. John can run **as fast as** Sam can. The traffic of Seoul is **as bad as** that of London.
not as + adjective/adverb + as	Korea is **not as large as** Canada. (= Korea is smaller than Canada.) The landscape of Canada is **not as mountainous as** that of Korea.
as + many + plural noun + as as + much + uncountable noun + as	I have **as many books as** she has. He has **as much money as** Karl has.

Tip ◆ A is not as adjective/adverb as B
   = A is not comparative than B = B is comparative than A
   e.g.) He is not as rich as Shirley.
     = He is not richer than Shirley. = Shirley is richer than he is.

 Look at the chart and complete the sentences using "(not) as ~ as" and the given words. (Use present tense.)

	Price (million won)	Weight (tons)	Maximum Speed (km/h)
Sports Car	50	2	400
Bus	50	4	180
Taxi	30	2	180

1 The taxi _____is not as heavy as_____ the bus. (be, heavy)

2 The bus _____ the taxi. (can, travel, fast)

3 The sports car _____ the taxi. (be, heavy)

4 The taxi _____ the sports car. (be, expensive)

5 The sports car _____ the bus. (be, expensive)

6 The taxi _____ the sports car. (can, travel, fast)

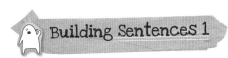

A Combine the sentences using "(not) as ~ as" and given words like the example.

Example Tom has $10. Mary has $5. (much)

↘ Mary ___ doesn't have as much money as ___ Tom has.

1 Chris is very tall. Cindy is quite short. (tall)

↘ Cindy _____ Chris.

2 Jamie has 200 books. Steve has 200 books, too. (many)

↘ Jamie _____ Steve has.

3 I drink a liter of water a day. Jenny also drinks a liter of water a day. (much)

↘ I _____ Jenny drinks.

4 The hospital is a seven-story building. The department store is a nine-story building. (tall)

↘ The hospital _____ the department store.

B Look at the pictures and write the sentences using the phrases in the box.

Word Box watch the baseball game   make many foreign friends   read many books
take this medicine   ~~visit Paris~~

1 I would recommend that you visit Paris.

2 _____

3 _____

4 _____

5 _____

 Put the words in the correct order to make a sentence.

Example	New York (is / exciting / an / place / live in / to).

↳ New York ___is an exciting place to live in___ .

1 She (write on / a piece of / to / paper / needs).

↳ She _____ .

2 There are (to / chairs / many / sit on).

↳ There are _____ .

3 Mike and Sam (write with / to / something / want).

↳ Mike and Sam _____ .

4 I'll be there if you (someone / need / talk with / to).

↳ I'll be there if you _____ .

5 He (many / play with / has / friends / to) because he is very active.

↳ He _____ because he is very active.

 Complete the essay using the phrases in the box.

Word Box	many attractions	as big as	the capital city
	would recommend	known for	enjoy the scenic view

I live in a city called Seoul, [1]_____ of South Korea.
Seoul is a great place to live in. In Seoul, there are [2]_____ : an
old palace called Gyeongbokgung, a tall structure called N Tower, a huge business and
entertainment center called COEX, and a soccer facility called Sangam Worldcup Stadium.
However, my favorite part is Insadong, which is [3]_____ its Korean
traditional tea shops. Seoul is [4]_____ New York, and you can
[5]_____ and learn Korean culture.
I [6]_____ that you visit Seoul as soon as possible because it is a
big and old city.

Writing

Brainstorming ‹Pair Work›

A Write an essay describing your hometown.

1 Where is your hometown? _____
(e.g. Auckland, the biggest city in New Zealand, Seoul, the capital of South Korea)

2 What is it like to live in? _____
(e.g. great, fantastic, exciting)

3 How many main attractions are there in your hometown? And what are they?

_____
(e.g. many, a few - fantastic zoo, the tallest building called Sky Tower, a huge park called Auckland Domain)

4 What is your favorite part of your hometown? And why is it your favorite part?

_____
(e.g. Westhaven Marina - the beautiful landscape, Central Park - Nature)

5 Tell more about your favorite place. _____
(e.g. known as the "City of Sails," because of a lot of boats)

6 Are there many things to do?   Yes ☐   No ☐

7 How is the atmosphere of your hometown? _____
(e.g. a quiet place to live in, a safe place to live in)

8 How is the nighttime atmosphere? Choose the phrase to describe nighttime at this place.

as quiet as a mouse ☐   as noisy as a truck ☐   as safe as houses ☐

as busy as a bee ☐   as dull as dishwater ☐   as good as it gets ☐

9 And how do you feel? _____
(e.g. easy to relax and rest in, comfortable to hang out)

10 Why would you recommend other people visit this place? _____
(e.g. clean, exciting, friendly)

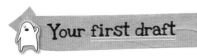

A Use your brainstorming to complete your draft. Look at the sample text and write your sentences in the same way.

Sample Text	Your Draft
Title	**Title**
My Hometown	My Hometown
Topic Sentence	**Topic Sentence**
I live in a city called Auckland, the biggest city in New Zealand.	1. _____
Body	**Body**
Auckland is a great place to live in.	2. _____
In Auckland, there are three main attractions: a small but fantastic zoo, the tallest structure called Sky Tower, and a huge park called Auckland Domain.	3. _____
However, my favorite part is Westhaven Marina because its landscape is beautiful. It is also known as the "City of Sails" because there are a lot of boats.	4, 5. _____
Even though there is so much to do, it is also a quiet place to live in.	6, 7. _____
At night, Auckland becomes as quiet as a mouse, so it is easy to rest and relax in.	8, 9. _____
Closing Sentence	**Closing Sentence**
I would recommend that you visit Auckland as soon as possible because it is a clean, exciting, and friendly city.	10. _____

Editing tips
- Remember to use "as ~ as" to show that two things or people are similar in some ways.
- Remember to use "to+base verb (+preposition)" like "to live in."

Writing Practice

Today is your birthday. Your parents have asked you to say what you want for a birthday gift, and they would buy it. Choose one of the illustrations, and write the response using the given words. Your response should be about 20 words and include two to three sentences.

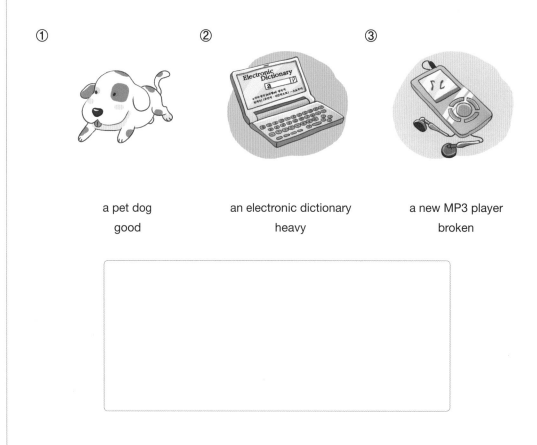

①	②	③
a pet dog	an electronic dictionary	a new MP3 player
good	heavy	broken

Unit 07

A Campaign Speech

Hello, everybody. My name is Kevin Terry. I have decided to run for school president. If I become the school president, I will do lots of good things for students. First of all, I will make sure that school food is fresh and good for our health. Second, I will also make sure that the swimming pool is clean. Next, I will build a suggestion box, so I will always be ready to listen to my fellow students. In addition, if you elect me, I will always be available to help you. Lastly, I will have a lot of fun after-school activities that every student can enjoy. If you vote for me, I will never let you down. Thank you for listening to my presentation, and I will now answer any questions you have.

A Campaign Speech

Warm-up

picture Description

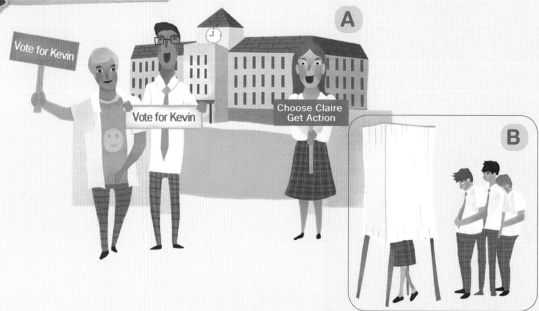

A Look at the pictures carefully and answer the questions using the given words.

1 In picture A, what are they doing? (run an election campaign)

⤷ They _____ to support candidates.

2 How many candidates are running for school president? (two)

⤷ _____

3 In picture B, why are the students standing in line? (to vote for the next school president)

⤷ They _____ .

B Look at the pictures carefully. Are these statements TRUE or FALSE?

1 Kevin and Claire are running for school president.　　　　　True ☐　　False ☐

2 Students know which candidate other students are voting for.　　True ☐　　False ☐

3 The students are standing in line and waiting for their turn to vote.　True ☐　　False ☐

Building Vocabulary

A Look at the pictures and complete the sentences using the given words.

Word Box	voting booth	pickets	ballot	slogan	candidate	campaign

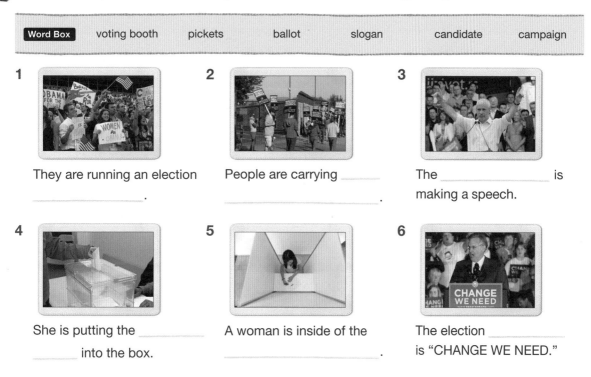

1 They are running an election _____ .

2 People are carrying _____ .

3 The _____ is making a speech.

4 She is putting the _____ into the box.

5 A woman is inside of the _____ .

6 The election _____ is "CHANGE WE NEED."

B Complete the sentences using the phrases in the box.

Word Box	win the election	cast a vote	takes place
	keeping his promise	vote against	run for

1 People over 18 have the right to _____ .

2 The politician was criticized for not _____ .

3 I will _____ him because I disagree with his ideas.

4 It's not easy to predict who will _____ this December.

5 The presidential election _____ every five years in Korea.

6 The mayor is popular among the young generation. I think he should _____ President.

Reading and Understanding

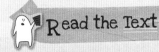

A Campaign Speech — Title

Hello, everybody. My name is Kevin Terry. — Introduction
I have decided to run for school president.

If I become the school president, I will do lots of good things for students. — Topic Sentence

First of all, I will make sure that school food is fresh and good for our health.

Second, I will also make sure that the swimming pool is clean. Next, I will build a

suggestion box, so I will always be ready to listen to my fellow students. In addition,

if you elect me, I will always be available to help you. Lastly, I will have a lot of

fun after-school activities that every student can enjoy.

Body

If you vote for me, I will never let you down. Thank you for listening to my

presentation, and I will now answer any questions you have.

Closing Remarks

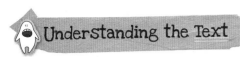
A Read the text and answer the questions like the example.

Example   What is the speaker's name?

↘ The speaker's name _____ is Kevin Terry _____.

1 What has Kevin decided to do?

↘ He _____.

2 What will he do to school food?

↘ He _____.

3 What will he do to the swimming pool?

↘ He _____.

4 Why does he want to build a suggestion box?

↘ He always wants to _____.

5 What will he have for every student to enjoy?

↘ He _____.

B Are these statements TRUE or FALSE?

1 Kevin Terry is one of the candidates for school president.   True ☐   False ☐

2 Kevin has promised two things to get students' votes.   True ☐   False ☐

3 If he is elected, he should be open to help students all the time.   True ☐   False ☐

4 The school president is chosen by teachers.   True ☐   False ☐

5 The students are not allowed to ask Kevin questions.   True ☐   False ☐

Complete the Outline

 Fill in the blanks to complete the outline.

Title -------- A Campaign Speech

: The title gives us the topic of the speech.

Introduction ----- Hello, everybody.

name: _____

decided to run for _____

: The introduction gives us a preview of the speech.

Topic Sentence ----- If I become _____.

: The topic sentence gives us the main idea of the speech.

Body -------- • First of all: make school food _____

| delicious and rich / fresh and healthy |

• Second: make the swimming pool _____

| clean / warm |

• Next: _____ to listen

| publish a school newsletter / build a suggestion box |

• In addition: always be available to _____

| help students / support teachers |

• Lastly: have a lot of fun _____

| after-school activities / study clubs |

: The body gives us the details about the speech.

Closing Remarks ----- - vote for me, _____

- thank you for _____

- _____ any questions you have

: The closing remarks summarize the speech, thanks us, and invites us to ask questions.

Grammar Point

> ● We use the first conditional to describe future events that are likely to happen.

If Clause	Main Clause
- condition	- result
- If + S + simple present	- S + will + base verb

Tip ♦ In this clause, we cannot use "will + base verb" instead of simple present tense.

If she **comes** to the party,	I **will be** very happy.
If I **study** hard,	I **will pass** the test.
If it**'s** sunny,	I**'ll go** for a walk.

Tip ♦ If "main clause" follows "if clause," a comma is needed between two clauses.
e.g.) If you cook, I will do the dishes.
If "if clause" follows "main clause," no comma is needed between two clauses.
e.g.) I will do the dishes if you cook.

A Complete the sentences using the words in the box.

Word Box	take	attend	ask	look	miss

1 If they invite me, I _____ the party.

2 If I see Rachel, I _____ her to call you.

3 If you don't hurry, you _____ the flight.

4 If I don't feel well tomorrow, I _____ a day off.

5 If you get your hair cut, you _____ completely different.

B Correct the errors and rewrite the sentences.

1 It will be cheaper if we will take the subway.

↳ _____

2 If I'll be late tonight, Mom will be very angry.

↳ _____

3 If you'll give me your address, I will send you an invitation.

↳ _____

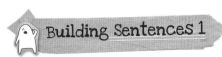 **Building Sentences 1**

 Look at the pictures and complete the sentences using the phrases in the box.

Word Box	never cross against the light	not tell your secret to anyone
	~~not cut in line~~	not run down the stairs

1 I _____ promise that I will not cut in line _____ .

2 I _____ .

3 I _____ .

4 I _____ .

B Complete the dialogs like the example.

Example	A: Take enough vitamin C.
	B: Don't worry! _I will make sure that I take enough vitamin C._

1 A: Finish your report this Friday.

B: Don't worry! _____

2 A: Return the books on time.

B: Don't worry! _____

3 A: Don't stay up late and play games.

B: Don't worry! _____

4 A: Turn off the light when you leave the office.

B: Don't worry! _____

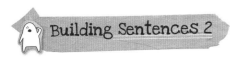
A Look at the pictures and complete the sentences using the given words.

1. _____ If it rains _____, I _____ will stay home _____.
   (rain, stay home)

2. _____, you _____.
   (exercise, lose weight)

3. _____, she _____.
   (eat a lot of sweets, get cavities)

4. _____, I _____.
   (walk to school, be late for school)

5. _____, he _____.
   (practice playing the piano hard, win a prize in the contest)

B Complete the essay using the phrases in the box.

Word Box	do class activities vote for	to lead and make running for	am good at organizing a hard-working person

Hello, everyone.

My name is Jennifer Jones. I'm [1] _____ class president.

I want to be a class president because I want [2] _____ our class the best in school!

First of all, I'm [3] _____, so I will do my best to help you and our teacher. Second, I'm a well-organized person. I [4] _____, and it will definitely help our class plan to [5] _____ like a bazaar. Lastly, I'm open-minded. I will listen carefully to your concerns.

If you [6] _____ me, I will make our class the best in school.

Thank you for listening.

Writing

 Brainstorming ‹Pair Work›

A Write a campaign speech.

1 What's your name? _____

2 What have you decided to run for? _____

(e.g. mayor, president, school president)

3 Write a topic sentence.

_____

(e.g. If I become the student president, I'll do a lot of good things for students.)

4 Talk about what you can do to achieve the position in detail.

First of all, _____

(e.g. make school food fresh and good, make the swimming pool clean, build a suggestion box, be always helpful, have a lot of fun after-school activities)

Second, _____

(e.g. make school food fresh and good, make the swimming pool clean, build a suggestion box, be always helpful, have a lot of fun after-school activities)

Next, _____

(e.g. make school food fresh and good, make the swimming pool clean, build a suggestion box, be always helpful, have a lot of fun after-school activities)

In addition, _____

(e.g. make school food fresh and good, make the swimming pool clean, build a suggestion box, be always helpful, have a lot of fun after-school activities)

Lastly, _____

(e.g. make school food fresh and good, make the swimming pool clean, build a suggestion box, be always helpful, have a lot of fun after-school activities)

5 What do you want to say to your listener? Write your own closing remarks.

_____

(e.g. If you vote for me, I will never let you down. Thank you for listening to my presentation, and I will now answer any questions you have.)

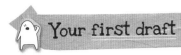

A Use your brainstorming to complete your draft. Look at the sample text and write your sentences in the same way.

Sample Text	Your Draft
Title	**Title**
A Campaign Speech	A Campaign Speech
Introduction	**Introduction**
Hello, everybody. My name is Kevin Terry. I have decided to run for school president.	1. 2.
Topic Sentence	**Topic Sentence**
If I become the school president, I will do lots of good things for students.	3.
Body	**Body**
First of all, I will make sure that school food is fresh and good for our health. Second, I will also make sure that the swimming pool is clean. Next, I will build a suggestion box, so I will always be ready to listen to the students. In addition, if you elect me, I will always be available to help you. Lastly, I will have a lot of fun after-school activities that every student can enjoy.	4.
Closing Remarks	**Closing Remarks**
If you vote for me, I will never let you down. Thank you for listening to my presentation, and I will now answer any questions you have.	5.

Editing tips
- Make sure you use "if" clause correctly.
- Make sure you include a correct introduction and closing remarks of your speech.

Writing Practice

Writing Test

Look at pictures 1 and 2, and describe what you see. Then imagine and write what will happen next. (30~50 words)

①  ② ③

Word Count

Unit 08

Going Abroad

Dear Cousin Barry,

I'm coming to see you in New York in the summer! My mom said I can study English in New York. I will come and stay with you for six weeks! What a wonderful trip it will be! Can you take me to the Empire State Building? I really want to see the amazing view from the top! And of course, I want to see a Yankees baseball game. You know how much I love the Yankees! When I go to Yankee Stadium, I will buy a Yankees home jersey. I am really excited about coming to New York, and I can't wait to see you. Please send me an email as soon as you can. See you soon.

Sincerely yours,

Simon

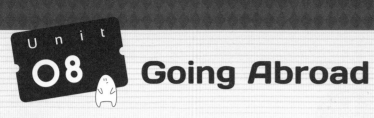

Going Abroad

Warm-up

Picture Description

GO YANKEES!

A Look at the picture carefully and answer the questions using the given phrases.

1 Where are the spectators now? (the baseball stadium)

↘ They _____ .

2 What are the spectators doing? (cheer for their favorite team)

↘ They _____ .

3 What is the batter doing on home plate? (wait for the pitcher to throw the ball)

↘ He _____ .

B Look at the picture carefully. Are these statements TRUE or FALSE?

1 The boy in a baseball uniform is holding a banner.   True ☐   False ☐

2 The batter just hit a home run, and the spectators go wild.   True ☐   False ☐

3 Some spectators are wearing baseball caps with the team logo.   True ☐   False ☐

A Look at the pictures and complete the sentences using the words in the box.

Word Box   souvenir   boarding pass   cart   passport   carousel   aisle seat

1
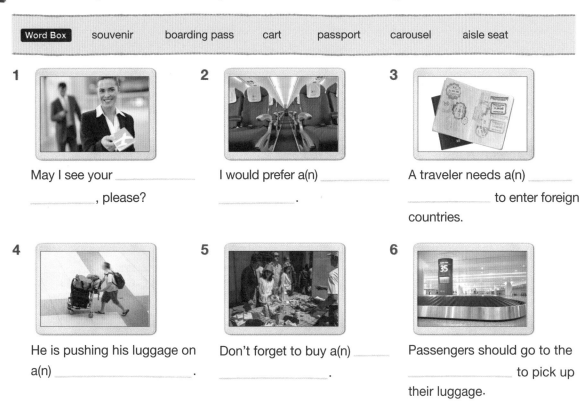

May I see your _____ _____, please?

2

I would prefer a(n) _____ _____.

3

A traveler needs a(n) _____ _____ to enter foreign countries.

4

He is pushing his luggage on a(n) _____.

5

Don't forget to buy a(n) _____.

6

Passengers should go to the _____ to pick up their luggage.

B Complete the sentences using the words in the box.

Word Box   bed and breakfast   confirm   peak season   book   passengers   travel agent

1 _____ is a private home which takes in guests.

2 It is often very expensive to travel during the _____.

3 I would like to _____ my reservation on Flight 337.

4 We need to _____ a hotel and buy our plane tickets.

5 It would be better to use a _____ to get great deals on hotels.

6 All _____ should prepare a valid passport and other travel documents at all times.

Reading and Understanding

R ead the Text

I'm Coming to New York!

Title

Greeting

Dear Cousin Barry,

I'm coming to see you in New York in the summer!

My mom said I can study English in New York. I will come and stay with

you for six weeks! What a wonderful trip it will be!

Can you take me to the Empire State Building? I really want to see the amazing

view from the top!

And of course, I want to see a Yankees baseball game. You know how much I

love the Yankees! When I go to Yankee Stadium, I will buy a Yankees home jersey.

I am really excited about coming to New York, and I can't wait to see you.

Please send me an email as soon as you can.

See you soon.

Email
Contents

Sincerely yours,

Simon

Sign-off

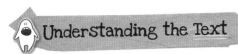

A Read the text and answer the questions like the example.

Example   Which sports team does Simon love? (the Yankees baseball team)

↘ Simon _____ loves the Yankees baseball team _____ .

---

1 What is Simon going to do in New York? (study English)

↘ Simon _____ .

2 How long will Simon stay with Barry? (for six weeks)

↘ Simon will _____ .

3 What does Simon want to see? (the view from the Empire State Building)

↘ Simon _____ .

4 Where does Simon want to go? (Yankee Stadium)

↘ Simon _____ .

5 How does Simon feel about coming to New York? (really excited)

↘ Simon _____ .

B Are these statements TRUE or FALSE?

1 Barry has sent a letter to his cousin Simon by mail.   True ☐   False ☐

2 Simon's mom didn't allow him to study in New York.   True ☐   False ☐

3 Simon will stay with Barry in New York during the summer.   True ☐   False ☐

4 Simon will visit the Statue of Liberty and see the amazing   True ☐   False ☐
view from the top.

5 Simon loves the Yankees and hopes to see a Yankees   True ☐   False ☐
baseball game.

Complete the Outline

 Fill in the blanks to complete the outline.

Title ------- I'm coming to New York!

: The title gives us the topic of the email.

Greeting ------- Dear _____,

: The greeting is the way to say hello to the person you are writing to.

Email Contents -------

• Purpose:
  - to see you and _____ | play baseball / study English |

• Where to go:
  - _____ | New York / London |

• When to go:
  - _____ | next week / this summer |

• Duration
  - _____ | six weeks / six days |

• What to do:
  - _____ the Empire State Building | to visit / to take |
  - _____ the amazing view from there | to visit / to see |
  - _____ a Yankees baseball game | to play / to see |
  - _____ a Yankees home jersey | to buy / to wait |

• Closing
Please _____.
See you soon.

: The email contents give us the details of what you want to write about.

Sign-off ------- Sincerely yours,

_____ (Writer's Name)

: The sign-off is the way to say goodbye to the person you are writing to.

Grammar Point

- We often use "to infinitive (to+base verb)" as an object or a complement and also to state our purposes.

Usages	Examples
Subject	**To study** a foreign language is interesting. = It is interesting **to study** a foreign language.
Object	I want **to visit** my hometown again.
Complement	My dream is **to travel** around the world. (my dream = to travel around the world)
Purpose	Sam studies hard **to teach** students well. (to teach = in order to teach)

 Correct the errors and rewrite the sentences.

1 I am planning to reading this book tomorrow.

➜ _____

2 She went to New York in order to studies English.

➜ _____

3 One of my close friends wants to is a professor.

➜ _____

 Combine the sentences using "to infinitive" like the example.

Example	I got up early in the morning. I wanted to catch the first train.
	➜ I got up early in the morning to catch the first train.

1 I went to Hong Kong. I wanted to meet my family.

➜ _____

2 I will turn on the computer. I want to play games.

➜ _____

3 A student is studying hard. He wants to get good grades on the midterms.

➜ _____

A Complete the sentences using the words in the box.

Word Box	clean	soon	~~fast~~	quiet	long	high	much

1 He ran _____as fast as possible_____ , and he won the race.

2 Keep your room _____ .

3 Children love to swing _____ .

4 Most people want to live _____ .

5 Please send me an ambulance _____ .

6 You should remain _____ in the library.

7 I went to a buffet restaurant for dinner and ate _____ .

B Look at the pictures and complete the sentences using the phrases in the box.

Word Box	lose weight	catch a ball	~~buy new jeans~~	get up early	be a pianist

1 I went to a clothing store _____to buy new jeans_____ .

2 A baseball player is running _____ .

3 You need to exercise more _____ .

4 She needs to practice harder _____ .

5 He set his alarm clock _____ in the morning.

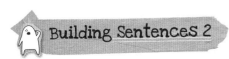
Building Sentences 2

A Look at the pictures and complete the sentences using the phrases in the box.

Word Box	learn ballet	have one's birthday party	~~come to Rome~~	buy a new car

1 I _____ am really excited about coming to Rome _____ .

2 She _____ .

3 He _____ .

4 She _____ .

B Complete the essay using the phrases in the box.

Word Box	it will be	how much I love	as soon as
	excited about	to visit you	love to ride

Dear Peter,

I'm planning ¹_____ in London in March! I'm going to stay in England for 10 days! What a wonderful trip ²_____!

Can you take me to the London Eye? I'd ³_____ on it and enjoy the beautiful scenery of London. I want to see an Arsenal FC soccer game. You know ⁴_____ Arsenal FC.

I am really ⁵_____ coming to England, and I can't wait to see you.

Please reply to my email ⁶_____ you can.

Best regards,

Susie

Writing

 Brainstorming ‹Pair Work›

A Write an email to someone informing him/her of your visit.

1 Which town or country will you visit? _____

2 What is the name of the person you will visit? _____

3 When will you visit? _____

4 Who said you can go? _____
   (e.g. Mom, Dad, the school principal)

5 What is the reason you are going? _____
   (e.g. soccer camp, ballet school, to relax, to study)

6 How long will you stay? _____
   (e.g. days, weeks, months, years)

7 What do you think the trip will be like? _____
   (e.g. wonderful, amazing, fantastic)

8 Where do you want the person to take you? Why?

   _____
   (e.g. the Eiffel Tower - to take some pictures, Buckingham Palace - to see the Queen)

9 What else do you want to do? Why?

   _____
   (e.g. to visit a museum - want to know about history, to go to the beach - love to swim in the sea)

10 What is your overall opinion about this trip? _____
   (e.g. excited, afraid but expectant, cheerful)

11 Write your own closing.

   _____
   (e.g. Please send me an email as soon as you can., See you soon.)

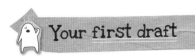

A Use your brainstorming to complete your draft. Look at the sample text and write your sentences in the same way.

Sample Text	Your Draft
Title	**Title**
I'm Coming to New York!	1. _____
Greeting	**Greeting**
Dear Cousin Barry,	2. _____
Email Contents	**Email Contents**
I'm coming to see you in New York in the summer! My mom said I can study English in New York. I will come and stay with you for six weeks! What a wonderful trip it will be! Can you take me to the Empire State Building? I really want to see the amazing view from the top! And of course, I want to see a Yankees baseball game. You know how much I love the Yankees! When I go to Yankee Stadium, I will buy a Yankees home jersey. I am really excited about coming to New York, and I can't wait to see you. Please send me an email as soon as you can. See you soon.	1, 3. _____ 4, 5. _____ 6. _____ 7. _____ 8. _____ 9. _____ 10. _____ 11. _____
Sign-off	**Sign-off**
Sincerely yours, Simon	_____ _____ (Writer's Name)

Editing tips

- Use exclamations to show surprise, emotion, or strong feelings.
- If your receiver is a boy, use "he/his." If your receiver is a girl, use "she/her."
- The exclamation mark "!" always comes at the end of the sentence.

Writing Practice

Writing Test

Look at the picture carefully and describe what people are doing.

There are some people in the clinic.

A boy and his mom _____(1)_____.

A nurse with a white cap _____(2)_____.

A woman at the front desk _____(3)_____.

A girl in a blue shirt _____(4)_____.

Word Count

(1)

(2)

(3)

(4)

Unit 09

My Favorite Website

I would like to introduce my favorite website, which is called www.goodthings1.com. I enjoy shopping online more than anything else in the world! So I was very happy when I discovered www.goodthings1.com about two months ago. This site sells a variety of clothes and accessories. And this website is special because the clothes and accessories are beautiful and cheap. Many people say that this website has correct and accurate information, and is up-to-date. I also like this site because I feel that surfing it is fun and interesting. Thanks to this website, I can save both money and time. I think this website is the best because it helps me buy clothes easily.

Unit 09 My Favorite Website

Warm-up

 Picture Description

A Look at the picture carefully and answer the questions using given phrases.

1 What is the woman doing? (buy clothes and accessories online)

↘ She _____ .

2 What is the man wearing on the screen? (black jeans and a black jacket)

↘ He _____ .

3 How much discount can the woman get? (a 30% discount)

↘ She _____ .

B Look at the picture carefully. Are these statements TRUE or FALSE?

1 The man is using his credit card to buy an item online.　　True ☐　　False ☐

2 The website sells clothes and accessories at discount prices.　　True ☐　　False ☐

3 The woman on the screen is wearing a necklace and sunglasses.　　True ☐　　False ☐

Building Vocabulary

A Look at the pictures and complete the sentences using the words in the box.

Word Box | on display | try on | get a refund | gift wrapping | browsing | discount

1
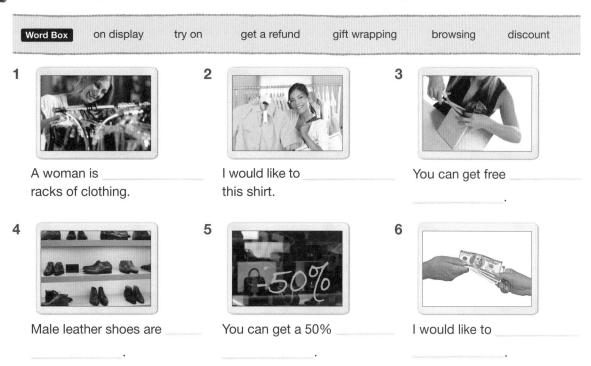
A woman is _____
racks of clothing.

2
I would like to _____
this shirt.

3
You can get free _____
_____ .

4
Male leather shoes are _____
_____ .

5
You can get a 50% _____
_____ .

6
I would like to _____
_____ .

B Complete the sentences using the phrases in the box.

Word Box | place an order online | track your order | is no longer available
| cancel my order | add it to the shopping cart | get free shipping

1 I would like to _____ due to the late delivery.

2 You can change the quantities after you _____ .

3 Sorry, the item you are trying to purchase _____ .

4 You can _____ by credit card through our online store.

5 You can _____ on orders over $30 to anywhere in Canada.

6 If you want to _____ , click the "My Account" or "Order Status" icon.

Reading and Understanding

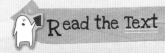 **R**ead the **T**ext

 My Favorite Website   Title

Topic Sentence

I would like to introduce my favorite website, which is called www.goodthings1.com.

I enjoy shopping online more than anything else in the world!

So I was very happy when I discovered www.goodthings1.com about two months ago.

This site sells a variety of clothes and accessories. And this website is special because the clothes and accessories are beautiful and cheap. Many people say that this website has correct and accurate information, and is up-to-date. I also like this site because I feel that surfing it is fun and interesting.

Thanks to this website, I can save both money and time.

Body I think this website is the best because it helps me buy clothes easily.

Closing Sentence

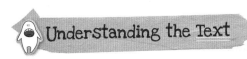

 Read the text and answer the questions like the example.

Example   What is your favorite website called?

↘ My favorite website _____ is called www.goodthings1.com _____ .

---

1 What do you enjoy most?

↘ I _____ .

2 When did you discover the website?

↘ I _____ .

3 Why is the website special?

↘ This website is special because _____ .

4 What do many people say about this website?

↘ They say this website has _____ .

5 Thanks to this website, what can you save?

↘ I _____ .

B **Are these statements TRUE or FALSE?**

1 The website has a few different products.   True ☐   False ☐

2 Surfing this website can be very interesting.   True ☐   False ☐

3 You can buy beautiful clothes on this website.   True ☐   False ☐

4 Most of the products on the website are highly expensive.   True ☐   False ☐

5 Many people believe this website gives the latest information.   True ☐   False ☐

Complete the Outline

 Fill in the blanks to complete the outline.

Title ------ My _____

: The title gives us the topic of the essay.

Topic Sentence ------ I would like _____ .

: The topic sentence gives us the main idea of the essay.

Body - - - - - - -

• What I enjoy most: _____

> online shopping / online games

• A useful website: www.goodthings1.com

• When I discovered: 2 months ago

• Why I like

- _____ products   a few / various

- beautiful and _____   cheap / expensive

- correct and _____ information   accurate / common

- _____   up-to-date / out of date

- _____ to surf   fast / fun and interesting

- _____ money and time   save / spend

: The body of the essay gives us the details about the topic.

Closing Sentence ------ I think _____

_____ .

: The closing sentence finishes the essay. It can be a statement or an opinion.

Grammar Point

> **You can make a gerund by adding "-ing" to verbs.**
>
> e.g.) saying, loving, hitting, studying, swimming, living, etc.
>
> **Tip** ◆ Verbs ending with "e": Remove "e" and add "-ing." e.g.) give ⇨ giving, save ⇨ saving
> Verbs ending with "ie": Remove "ie" and add "-ying." e.g.) die ⇨ dying, lie ⇨ lying
> Verbs ending with "short vowel + consonant": Double the short vowel and add "-ing."
> e.g.) plan ⇨ planning, clap ⇨ clapping
>
> **You can use a gerund as a subject and an object, and also after prepositions.**
>
> | Usages | Examples |
> |---|---|
> | Gerunds as Subjects | **Surfing** this site is fun and interesting.
Exercising is very helpful for your health. |
> | Gerunds as Objects | She enjoys **reading** comic books.
(mind, enjoy, finish, keep, give up + gerund) |
> | Gerunds after Prepositions | Jane is very good at **swimming**.
How about **watching** a movie tonight? |

Correct the errors and rewrite the sentences.

1 Henry is interested in danceing and singing.

↘ _____

2 He usually enjoys swiming in the morning.

↘ _____

3 Tom kept plays the piano, and it annoyed me.

↘ _____

4 She is going to spend her vacation studing math.

↘ _____

Complete the sentences using the gerunds of the words in the box.

Word Box	come	write	spend	cook

1 Thank you for _____ to my birthday party.

2 My son enjoys _____ time with his pet dog.

3 My wife is very good at _____, and we seldom eat out.

4 Jamie finished _____ a fan letter to his favorite sports hero.

 A Complete the sentences using the given words like the example.

| Example | I would like to introduce _my favorite website_ , _which is called www.goodthings1.com_ .
(website, www.goodthings1.com) |

1 I would like to introduce _____ , _____ .
(sport, soccer)

2 I would like to introduce _____ , _____ .
(country, Italy)

3 I would like to introduce _____ , _____ .
(mountains, the Rockies)

4 I would like to introduce _____ , _____ .
(book, *Pride and Prejudice*)

5 I would like to introduce _____ , _____ .
(movie, *The Chronicles of Narnia*)

B Look at the pictures and write the sentences like the example.

| Example | bed | Thanks to beds, we can sleep soundly.
(sleep soundly) |

1 microwave _____
(heat up food easily)

2 refrigerator _____
(keep food and drinks cold)

3 the Internet _____
(make friends from across the world)

4 airplane _____
(travel around the world in one or two days)

Building Sentences 2

A Look at the pictures and complete the sentences like the example.

Example

I ___enjoy playing tennis more than anything else in the world___ !
(play tennis)

1

She _____ !
(ski)

2

She _____ !
(ride a bike)

3

I _____ !
(read books)

4

I _____ !
(run)

5

He _____ !
(watch a basketball game)

B Complete the essay using the phrases in the box.

Word Box	various kinds of	read books everywhere	would like to introduce
	thanks to	more than anything else	build my knowledge

I [1]_____ my favorite website, which is called www.favoritebooks.com.

I enjoy reading books [2]_____ in the world! So I was very excited when

I discovered www.favoritebooks.com. This site has lots of e-books. Many people said that

this website is good because there are [3]_____ e-books, and it also has

audio books. [4]_____ this website, I can [5]_____

from various books.

I think this website is the best because I can [6]_____ .

111

Writing

A Write your review on your favorite website.

1 What is your favorite website? _____

2 What do you enjoy doing online most? _____

(e.g. shopping online, playing games, reading news and discussing it)

3 When did you discover this website? And how did you feel then?

_____

(e.g. yesterday - happy, two months ago - excited, a long time ago - surprised)

4 What does this website do? Or what is on this website?

_____

(e.g. sells a variety of clothes and accessories, gives me lots of news about the world)

5 Why is this website special? _____

(e.g. beautiful and cheap clothes, up-to-date information, unbiased news)

6 What do other people say about this website?

_____

(e.g. has correct and accurate information, has many users, offers plenty of different reviews)

7 Why else do you like this website?

_____

(e.g. fun and interesting to surf, discuss the stories with others, play games, use free email)

8 Thanks to this website, what can you do? _____

(e.g. save money and time, share my opinions with others, know the latest news, learn English)

9 Why do you think this website is the best? _____

(e.g. helps me buy clothes easily, helps me learn about the world, helps me learn English)

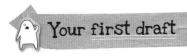
Your first draft

A Use your brainstorming to complete your draft. Look at the sample text and write your sentences in the same way.

Sample Text	Your Draft
Title	**Title**
My Favorite Website	My Favorite Website
Topic Sentence	**Topic Sentence**
I would like to introduce my favorite website, which is called www.goodthings1.com.	1.
Body	**Body**
I enjoy shopping online more than anything else in the world!	2.
So I was very happy when I discovered www.goodthings1.com about two months ago.	3.
This site sells a variety of clothes and accessories.	4.
	5.
And this website is special because the clothes and accessories are beautiful and cheap.	6.
Many people say that this website has correct and accurate information and is up-to-date.	7.
I also like this site because I feel that surfing it is fun and interesting.	8.
Thanks to this website, I can save both money and time.	
Closing Sentence	**Closing Sentence**
I think this website is the best because it helps me buy clothes easily.	9.

> **Editing tips**
> - Remember that every gerund ends in "-ing," but it functions as a noun.
> - You can use a gerund as a subject, a complement, or an object of a sentence.

Writing Practice

Writing Test

Tomorrow is a holiday. You want to do something very exciting with your friend. Choose one of the illustrations, and write the reason you chose it using the given words. Your answer should be about 20 words and include two to three sentences. (20~30 words)

① watch a movie
like

② go to an amusement park
ride

③ go hiking
exercise

Word Count

Unit
10

A Complaint Letter

Dear Mr. Green,

My name is Michael Jones. I have really enjoyed listening to classical music through your radio station for many years. But now I am writing to complain because your station does not play classical music anymore. I know that a lot of people like pop music nowadays, so I understand your station needs to play it. But I really want to listen to classical music again through your radio station, and many of my friends like classical music, too. I have asked for classical songs by emailing your radio station many times. However, your station has never played my requested songs, so I am asking you to accept my request to hear some classical music. Thank you for reading my complaint letter. I look forward to receiving your reply.

Sincerely yours,

Michael Jones

Warm-up

Picture Description

A Look at the pictures carefully and answer the questions using the given words.

1 What is the boy writing? (a complaint letter)

↳ He _____ .

2 Why did he feel very upset? (find, the lens of the digital camera was broken)

↳ He _____ because _____ .

3 What is the girl writing? (a thank-you note)

↳ She _____ .

4 Why did she feel so pleased? (receive, a pair of pretty shoes)

↳ She _____ because _____ .

B Look at the pictures carefully. Are these statements TRUE or FALSE?

1 The boy who is writing a letter is not happy.   True ☐   False ☐

2 The boy ordered the digital camera on the Internet.   True ☐   False ☐

3 The girl got a pair of new shoes from her grandmother.   True ☐   False ☐

A Look at the pictures and complete the sentences using the phrases in the box.

Word Box | a bad dish | the flight delay | ~~the noise~~
| a bad haircut | high prices | a poor-quality product

1

A woman is complaining about ___the noise___ .

2

A guest is complaining about _____ .

3

A shopper is complaining about _____ .

4

A customer is complaining about _____ .

5

A man is complaining about _____ .

6

A girl is complaining about _____ .

B Complete the sentences using the phrases in the box.

Word Box | a thank-you note | an invitation card | complaint letters
| an apology letter | a get-well-soon card | a good-luck card

1 Her wedding is one month away. She is writing _____ .

2 Her grandmother sent her a nice present. She is writing _____ .

3 He had an argument with his friend last night. He is writing _____ to her.

4 My uncle is sick in the hospital. I am writing _____ to make him feel better.

5 The manager received _____ because the service at the restaurant was terrible.

6 He is writing _____ to his sister because she is taking her college entrance examinations tomorrow.

Reading and Understanding

 Read the Text

A Complaint Letter　　　Title

Dear Mr. Green,　　Greeting

My name is Michael Jones.

I have really enjoyed listening to classical music through your radio station for many years. But now I am writing to complain because your station does not play classical music anymore.

I know that a lot of people like pop music nowadays, so I understand your station needs to play it. But I really want to listen to classical music again through your radio station, and many of my friends like classical music, too. I have asked for classical songs by emailing your radio station many times. However, your station has never played my requested songs, so I am asking you to accept my request to hear some classical music.

Thank you for reading my complaint letter. I look forward to receiving your reply.

Sincerely yours,

Michael Jones　　Sign-off

Letter Contents

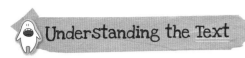
 A Read the text and answer the questions like the example.

Example Who is Michael Jones writing to?

↘ He _____ is writing to Mr. Green .

1 What did Michael Jones really enjoy?

↘ He really _____ .

2 Why is Michael Jones writing this letter?

↘ He is writing to _____ because the radio station _____ .

3 What type of music do a lot of people like nowadays?

↘ A lot of people _____ .

4 What is Michael Jones asking Mr. Green to accept?

↘ He is asking Mr. Green _____ .

5 What does Michael Jones look forward to?

↘ He _____ .

B Are these statements TRUE or FALSE?

1 Michael Jones has written to Mr. Green at the radio station.　　True ☐　　False ☐

2 Michael Jones wants to listen to classical music less.　　True ☐　　False ☐

3 The radio station always plays lots of pop music.　　True ☐　　False ☐

4 Michael Jones has never emailed the radio station.　　True ☐　　False ☐

5 Michael Jones wants to receive a response from the radio station.　　True ☐　　False ☐

Complete the Outline

 Fill in the blanks to complete the outline.

Title ----- _____

: The title gives us the topic of the letter.

Greeting ----- _____,

: The greeting is the way to say hello to the person you are writing to.

Letter Contents -----

Introduction

- Who I am:　　　　Michael Jones
- What I did:　　　enjoyed _____ classical music

   [playing / listening to]

- Reason to write: _____ [to complain / to praise]

Details

- a lot of people like _____ [classical music / pop music]

- I want to listen to _____ [classical music / pop music]

- I have asked for _____ [classical songs / pop songs]

- the station never has played my _____

   [pop songs / requested songs]

- I am asking _____ my request [to refuse / to accept]

Closing

Thank you for _____ .

I look forward to _____ .

: The letter contents give us details of what you want to write about.

Sign-off -----

_____

_____

: The sign-off is the way to say goodbye to the person you are writing to.

Grammar Point

A quantifier is a word or a phrase that shows the amount or quantity. "Much," "many," and "a lot of" indicate a large quantity of something.

many	much	a lot of
"Many" is used with plural countable nouns.	"Much" is used with uncountable nouns. **Tip** ◆ It is usually used a negative sentence and a question.	"A lot of" is used with both plural countable and uncountable nouns.
many <u>books</u> **many** <u>movies</u>	**much** <u>food</u> **much** <u>gas</u>	**a lot of** <u>books</u> **a lot of** <u>movies</u> **a lot of** <u>gas</u>
I have **many** <u>friends</u>. I don't have **many** <u>friends</u>.	I don't have **much** <u>money</u>. Do you gain **much** <u>weight</u> on holiday?	I have **a lot of** <u>friends</u>. I don't have **a lot of** <u>friends</u>. I have **a lot of** <u>money</u>. I don't have **a lot of** <u>money</u>.

Tip ◆ A few (for countable nouns) and a little (for uncountable nouns) show quantity or amount in a positive way.
   e.g.) a few books (not many but enough), a little money (not much but enough)
   Few (for countable nouns) and little (for uncountable nouns) show quantity or amount in a negative way.
   e.g.) few people (almost no people), little money (almost no money)

A Fill in the blanks using "many" or "much."

1 Let's go. We don't have _____ time.

2 I don't read very much. I don't have _____ books.

3 How _____ times do you go to the movies a week?

4 There are _____ people in this room. It's hard to get in.

B Rewrite the sentences using "many" or "much."

1 I drink a lot of glasses of water every day.

   ↘ _____

2 He doesn't have a lot of homework to do today.

   ↘ _____

3 Do you get a lot of advice about studying from your teacher?

   ↘ _____

A Look at the pictures and complete the sentences using the words in the box.

| Word Box | many | a little | few | much | a few | little |

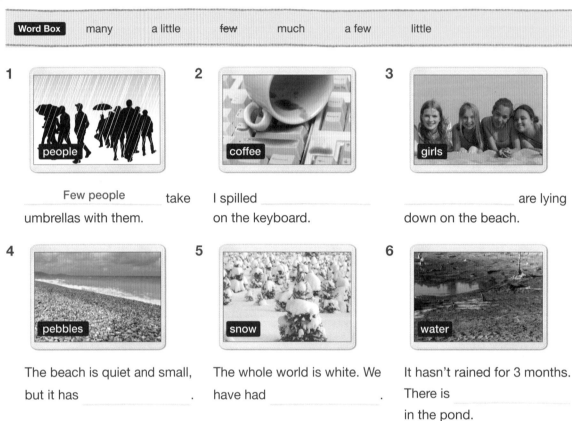

1
people

_____Few people_____ take umbrellas with them.

2
coffee

I spilled _____ on the keyboard.

3
girls

_____ are lying down on the beach.

4
pebbles

The beach is quiet and small, but it has _____.

5
snow

The whole world is white. We have had _____.

6
water

It hasn't rained for 3 months. There is _____ in the pond.

B Complete the sentences like the example.

| Example | He _____used to watch TV_____ a lot, but he doesn't watch TV much anymore. |

1 I _____ a lot of _____, but I don't eat much fast food anymore.

2 My mom _____, but she doesn't have long hair anymore.

3 He _____, but he doesn't play computer games anymore.

4 My neighbor _____, but she doesn't have a dog anymore.

5 My uncle _____, but he doesn't run a bike shop anymore.

6 My family _____, but we don't eat out often anymore.

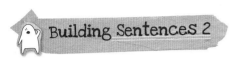

Building Sentences 2

A Look at the pictures and write the sentences using the phrases in the box.

Word Box
apply for a job as a teacher
thank you for your wonderful present

request a refund for a pair of jeans
~~invite you to my birthday party~~

1

I'm writing to invite you to my birthday party.

2

_____

3

_____

4

_____

B Complete the essay using the phrases in the box.

Word Box
do anything
am writing to

your reply
many times

wasn't cleaned
get my money back

Dear Hotel Manager,

I ¹_____ complain about your hotel's service.

The bread wasn't fresh, and the milk already passed its expiration date. In addition, the room ²_____ at all. I told the clerk at the front desk all of those things ³_____, but he didn't ⁴_____. I would like to ⁵_____ since I didn't stay even a day.

Thank you for reading my complaint letter. I look forward to ⁶_____.

Sincerely yours,
Jamie Brown

Writing

 Brainstorming ‹Pair Work›

A Write a complaint letter.

1 Who are you writing to?

_____
(e.g. restaurant manager, store clerk, customer service)

2 What's your name?

_____

3 What have you done? Or what did you do?

_____
(e.g. stayed many times, ordered a product often)

4 Why are you writing to complain?

_____
(e.g. the staff didn't listen to me, the product is broken)

5 What do/did you know about the problem? So, what do/did you understand?

_____
(e.g the computer system broke down - your staff was confused,
the volume of orders is larger - the clerk could make a mistake)

6 But what do/did you really want to do? And what have you done?

_____
(e.g. to listen to classical music - asked for classical songs,
to exchange it for a new one - called customer service)

7 However, what happened to you? So, what do you ask them to do for you?

_____
(e.g. didn't believe me - listen to your customers, didn't exchange it for a new one - send a proper product)

8 Write your own closing of your complaint letter.

_____
(e.g. Thank you for reading my complaint letter., I look forward to receiving your reply.)

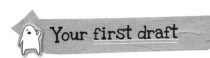

A Use your brainstorming to complete your draft. Look at the sample text and write your sentences in the same way.

Sample Text	Your Draft
Title	**Title**
A Complaint Letter	_____
Greeting	**Greeting**
Dear Mr. Green,	1. _____
Letter Contents	**Letter Contents**
My name is Michael Jones. I have really enjoyed listening to classical music through your radio station for many years. But now I am writing to complain because your station does not play classical music anymore. I know that a lot of people like pop music nowadays, so I understand your station needs to play it. But I really want to listen to classical music again through your radio station, and many of my friends like classical music, too. I have asked for classical songs by emailing your radio station many times. However, your station has never played my requested songs, so I am asking you to accept my request to hear some classical music. Thank you for reading my complaint letter. I look forward to receiving your reply.	2. _____ 3. _____ 4. _____ 5. _____ 6. _____ 7. _____ 8. _____
Sign-off	**Sign-off**
Sincerely yours, Michael Jones	_____ _____ (Writer's Name)

Editing tips
- Make sure you use "many," "much," and "a lot of" correctly.
- Make sure you include a correct greeting and sign-off in your letter.

Writing Practice

Writing Test

Your aunt visited your house to see you. However, you were away from home to attend a summer camp. Write a letter to your aunt saying that you are sorry for not seeing her. (about 30 words)

Subject : I miss you!

Dear Aunt Anny,

_____

_____

_____

_____

_____

_____

Josh

Word Count

Memo!

Memo!

수준별 맞춤

Vocabulary 시리즈

The VOCA+BULARY 완전 개정판 1~7

This Is Vocabulary 초급, 중급, 고급, 어원편

Grammar 시리즈

Grammar 공감 Level 1~3

After School Grammar Level 1~3

Grammar Bridge Level 1~3 개정판

중학영문법 뽀개기 Level 1~3

The Grammar with Workbook starter Level 1~2

OK Grammar Level 1~4

The Grammar Starter Level 1~3

This Is Grammar 초급 1·2 중급 1·2 고급 1·2

넥서스 중등 영어 시리즈

Reading 시리즈

Reading 공감 Level 1~3

After School Reading Level 1~3

THIS IS READING 1~4 전면 개정판

Smart Reading Basic Level 1~2
Smart Reading Level 1~2

Listening 시리즈

Listening 공감 Level 1~3

After School Listening Level 1~3

The Listening Level 1~4

도전! 만점 중학 영어듣기 모의고사 Level 1~3

공든탑 Listening 유형편, 적용편 실전모의고사 1·2

리스닝 본능 Level 1~4